IBM PC®
An Introduction to the Operating System, BASIC Programming and Applications

Revised and Enlarged

Dr. Larry Joel Goldstein
Martin Goldstein

Published by
Robert J. Brady Co.
A Prentice-Hall Publishing and
Communications Company
Bowie, MD 20715

IBM PC: An Introduction to the Operating System, BASIC Programming and Applications—Revised and Enlarged

Copyright © 1984 Robert J. Brady Co.
All rights reserved. No part of this publication may be reproduced or transmitted in any form or by any means, electronic or mechanical, including photocopying and recording, or by any information storage and retrieval system, without permission in writing from the publisher. For information, address Robert J. Brady Co., Bowie, Maryland 20715.

Library of Congress Cataloging in Publication Data

Goldstein, Larry Joel.
   IBM PC: an introduction to programming and applications.

  Bibliography: p.
  Includes index.
  1. IBM Personal Computer—Programming. 2. BASIC (Computer program language) I. Goldstein, Martin, 1919 Mar. 28-   . II. Title. III. I.B.M. P.C.
QA76.8.I2594GGG64   1983   001.64'2   83-11780
ISBN 0-89303-530-0

Prentice-Hall International, Inc., London
Prentice-Hall Canada, Inc., Scarborough, Ontario
Prentice-Hall of Australia, Pty., Ltd., Sydney
Prentice-Hall of India Private Limited, New Delhi
Prentice-Hall of Japan, Inc., Tokyo
Prentice-Hall of Southeast Asia Pte. Ltd., Singapore
Whitehall Books, Limited, Petone, New Zealand
Editora Prentice-Hall Do Brasil LTDA., Rio de Janeiro

Printed in the United States of America

85 86 87 88 89 90 91 92 93 94   10 9 8 7 6 5 4 3

Executive Editor: David T. Culverwell
Production Editor/Text Designer: Michael J. Rogers
Art Director/Cover Design: Don Sellers
Assistant Art Director: Bernard Vervin
Photography: George Dodson
Typefaces: Palatino (text), Eurostile (display), Special Digitized (computer programs)
Typesetting: Harper Graphics, Waldorf, MD
Printing: R. R. Donnelley & Sons Company, Harrisonburg, VA

Contents

I Getting Started With Your PC   1
- **1 A First Look at Computers**   3
  - 1.1 Introduction   4
  - 1.2 What is a Computer?   6
  - 1.3 A Grand Tour of Your IBM Personal Computer   9
  - 1.4 Typical PC Components and Systems   13
- **2 Using Your PC for the First Time**   19
  - 2.1 On Diskettes and Diskette Drives   20
  - 2.2 Starting Your PC   22
  - 2.3 More About Diskette Drives   25
  - 2.4 Backing Up Your DOS Diskette   26
  - 2.5 The Keyboard   28
- **3 An Introduction to DOS**   37
  - 3.1 Files and File Names   38
  - 3.2 File Specifications   41
  - 3.3 Executing Commands and Programs   43
  - 3.4 The COPY Command   45
  - 3.5 COPYing and FORMATting Diskettes   48
  - 3.6 Other DOS Internal Commands   51
  - 3.7 Other DOS External Commands   53
  - 3.8 Creating Your Own DOS Commands—Batch Files   54

II An Introduction to PC BASIC   59
- **4 Getting Started in BASIC**   61
  - 4.1 Beginning BASIC   62
  - 4.2 Running BASIC Programs   62
  - 4.3 Writing BASIC Programs   64
  - 4.4 Some Elementary BASIC Programs   67
  - 4.5 Giving Names to Numbers and Words   75
  - 4.6 Some BASIC Commands   84
  - 4.7 Some Programming Tips   91
  - 4.8 Using the BASIC Editor   91
- **5 Controlling the Flow of Your Program**   97
  - 5.1 Doing Repetitive Operations   98
  - 5.2 Letting Your Computer Make Decisions   109
  - 5.3 Structuring Solutions to Problems   122
  - 5.4 Subroutines   124
- **6 Working With Data**   133
  - 6.1 Working With Tabular Data—Arrays   134
  - 6.2 Inputting Data   141
  - 6.3 Formatting Your Output   147
  - 6.4 Gambling With Your Computer   155

7	**Easing Programming Frustrations**	**165**
	7.1 Flow Charting	166
	7.2 Errors and Debugging	169
	7.3 Some Common Error Messages	173
	7.4 Further Debugging Hints	174
8	**Your Computer as a File Cabinet**	**177**
	8.1 What Are Files?	178
	8.2 Sequential Files	179
	8.3 More About Sequential Files	188
	8.4 Random Access Files	191
	8.5 An Application of Random Access Files	197
	8.6 Sorting Techniques	202
	8.7 BASIC File Commands	206
9	**String Manipulation**	**211**
	9.1 ASCII Character Codes	212
	9.2 Operations on Strings	216
	9.3 Control Characters	221
	9.4 Printer Controls and Form Letters	224
10	**An Introduction to Computer Graphics**	**231**
	10.1 Line Graphics	232
	10.2 Drawing Bar Charts	241
	10.3 Computer Art	246
	10.4 Color and Graphics Modes	248
	10.5 Lines, Rectangles and Circles	254
	10.6 Drawing Pie Charts	261
	10.7 Sound and Music on the PC	264
	10.8 PAINT and DRAW	269
11	**Word Processing**	**279**
	11.1 What is Word Processing?	280
	11.2 Using Your Computer As a Word Processor	280
	11.3 A Do-It-Yourself Word Processor	282
12	**Some Additional Programming Tools**	**287**
	12.1 The INKEY$ Function	288
	12.2 The Function Keys and Event Trapping	289
	12.3 Error Trapping	294
	12.4 Chaining Programs	296
13	**Computer Games**	**299**
	13.1 Telling Time With Your Computer	300
	13.2 Blind Target Shoot	304
	13.3 Saving and Recalling Graphics Images	308
	13.4 Shooting Gallery	311
	13.5 Tic Tac Toe	314

14	**Different Kinds of Numbers in PC BASIC**	**321**
	14.1 Single- and Double-Precision Numbers	322
	14.2 Variable Types	327
	14.3 Mathematical Functions in BASIC	329
	14.4 Defining Your Own Functions	334
15	**Computer-Generated Simulations**	**337**
	15.1 Simulation	338
	15.2 Simulation of a Computer Store	340
16	**Software You Can Buy**	**345**
	16.1 A Survey of Software You Can Buy	346
	16.2 Spreadsheets	347
	16.3 Buying Software	351
17	**Some Other Applications of Your Computer**	**353**
	17.1 Computer Communications	354
	17.2 Advanced Graphics	356
	17.3 Connections to the Outside World	357
18	**Where To Go From Here**	**359**
	18.1 Assembly Language Programming	360
	18.2 Other Languages and Operating Systems	361
	18.3 Suggestions for Further Reading	362

Answers to Selected Exercises   **365**

Index   **389**

Documentation for Optional Program Diskette   **392**

Preface to the Second Edition

The IBM PC world has changed a great deal since the introduction of our first edition. DOS has undergone several revisions, the PC has come out with an expanded version, the PC/XT, and the capabilities of PC BASIC have been extended. This edition takes into account these profound changes.

We have taken this opportunity to expand the content of the book as follows:

- The book now begins with an extensive discussion of DOS. This is for the user who may not want to learn BASIC immediately but wishes to learn enough about the PC and DOS in order to run purchased programs.
- We give more tips on learning to program and how to develop programs in a structured fashion.
- We have expanded the discussion of graphics and included a section on sound.
- We have included discussions of function key usage, chaining programs, error trapping, and INKEY$.
- We have revised many programs and introduced many new ones.
- We have expanded the optional program diskette from 36 to 63 programs. To order this diskette, see your local dealer or use the attached order envelope.

Our goal in this edition remains the same as for the first edition: Providing a clear, motivated introduction to the PC, stressing applications.

Our sincere thanks go to all the readers who have taken the time to communicate with us and to share their ideas, their enthusiasm, and their frustration. Many of their ideas and suggestions have found their way into the book. Once again, we wish to express our deepest appreciation to all our friends at the Robert J. Brady Co. for their efforts which go well-beyond the call. Our special thanks to Mike Rogers and Tony Melendez for their guidance of the production process, to Jessie Katz for assistance in arranging for reviewers and for handling the flow of correspondence with our readers, to Don Sellers for his imaginative art work, to George Dodson for his beautiful photography, and to Joan Caldwell for her sales and promotion efforts. Last but not least, we would like to thank our close friends and associates, David Culverwell, Editor-in-Chief, and Harry Gaines, President, for their support and enthusiastic encouragement.

Dr. Larry Joel Goldstein
Martin Goldstein

Limits of Liability and Disclaimer of Warranty

The authors and publisher of this book have used their best efforts in preparing this book and the programs contained in it. These efforts include the development, research, and testing of the theories and programs to determine their effectiveness. The author and publisher make no warranty of any kind, expressed or implied, with regards to these programs or the documentation contained in this book. The authors and publisher shall not be liable in any event for incidental or consequential damages in connection with, or arising out of, the furnishing, performance, or use of these programs.

Trademarks of Material Mentioned in This Text

IBM PC and PC/XT are registered trademarks of International Business Machines Corporation.
Visicalc is a registered trademark of Visicorp, Inc.
CP/M-86 is a registered trademark of Digital Research Corporation.
UNIX is a registered trademark of Bell Telephone Laboratories, Inc.

NOTE TO AUTHORS

Do you have a manuscript or a software program related to personal computers? Do you have an idea for developing such a project? If so, we would like to hear from you. The Brady Co. produces a complete range of books and applications software for the personal computer market. We invite you to write to David Culverwell, Editor-in-Chief, Robert J. Brady Co., Bowie, MD 20715.

I

Getting Started With Your PC

A First Look at Computers 1

1.1 Introduction

The computer age is barely thirty years old, but it has already had a profound effect on all our lives. Indeed, computers are now prevalent in the office, the factory, and even the supermarket. In the last three or four years, the computer has even become commonplace in the home as people have purchased millions of computer games and millions of personal computers. Computers are so common today that it is hard to imagine even a single day in which a computer will not somehow affect us.

In spite of the explosion of computer use in our society, most people know very little about them. They view the computer as an "electronic brain," and do not know how a computer works, how it may be used, and how greatly it may simplify various everyday tasks. This does not reflect a lack of interest. Most people realize that computers are here to stay, and are interested in finding out how to use them. If you are so inclined, then this book is for you!

This book is an introduction to personal computing for the novice. You may be a student, teacher, homemaker, business person, or just a curious individual. We assume that you have had little or no previous exposure to computers and want to learn the fundamentals. We will guide you as you turn on your IBM PC for the first time. (There's really nothing to it!) From there, we will lead you through the fundamentals of talking with your computer in the BASIC language. Throughout, we will provide exercises for you to test your understanding of the material. We will show the many ways *you can use your computer*. The exercises will suggest programs you can write. Many of the exercises will be designed to give you insight into how computers are used in business and industry. We will suggest a number of applications of the computer within your home. For good measure we'll even build a few computer games!

What is Personal Computing?

In the early days of computing (the 1940s and 1950s), the typical computer was a huge mass of electronic parts which occupied several rooms. In those days, it was often necessary to reinforce the floor of a computer room, and to install special air conditioning so the computer could function properly. Moreover, an early computer was likely to cost several million dollars. Over the years, the cost of computers has decreased dramatically and, thanks to micro-miniaturization, their size has shrunk even faster than their price.

In the late 1970s, the first "personal" computers were put on the market. These computers were reasonably inexpensive and were designed to allow the average person to learn about the computer and to use it to solve everyday problems. These personal computers proved to be incredbly popular and have stirred the imaginations of people in all walks of life. It is no exaggeration to say that a computer revolution is now under way, as millions of people are learning to fit computers into their everyday lives.

The personal computer is not a toy. It is a genuine computer which has most of the features of its big brothers, the so-called "main-frame" computers, which still cost several million dollars. A personal computer can be equipped with enough capacity to handle the accounting and inventory control tasks of most small businesses. It can also perform computations for engineers and scientists, and it can even be used to keep track of home finances and personal clerical chores. It would be quite impossible to give a complete list of the possible applications of personal computers. However, the following list can suggest the range of possibilities:

For the business person
  Accounting
  Record keeping
  Clerical chores
  Inventory
  Cash management
  Payroll
  Graph and chart preparation
  Word processing
  Data analysis
  Networking

For the home
  Record keeping
  Budget management
  Investment analysis
  Correspondence
  Energy conservation
  Home security
  On-line information retrieval
  Tax return preparation

For the student
  Computer literacy
  Preparation of term papers
  Analysis of experiments
  Preparation of graphs and charts
  Project schedules
  Storage and organization of notes

For the professional
  Billing
  Analysis of data
  Report generation
  Correspondence

Stock market data access
Scientific/engineering calculations

For recreation
Computer games
Computer graphics
Computer art

As you can see, the list is quite extensive. If your interests aren't listed, don't worry! There's plenty of room for those of you who are just plain curious about computers and wish to learn about them as a hobby.

The IBM Personal Computer*

This book will introduce you to personal computing on the IBM Personal Computer, both the PC and PC/XT versions. This machine is an incredibly sophisticated device which incorporates many of the features of its "main-frame" big brothers. Before we begin to discuss these particular features of the IBM Personal Computer, let us begin by discussing the features found in all computers.

1.2 What is a Computer?

At the heart of every computer is a **central processing unit** (or **CPU**) which performs the commands you specify. This unit carries out arithmetic, makes logical decisions, and so forth. In essence, the CPU is the "brain" of the computer. The **memory** of a computer allows it to "remember" numbers, words, and paragraphs, as well as the list of commands you wish the computer to perform. The **input unit** allows you to send information to the computer; the **output unit** allows the computer to send information to you. The relationship of these four basic components of a computer are shown in Figure 1-1.

In an IBM Personal Computer the CPU is contained in a tiny electronic chip, called an **8088 microprocessor**. As a computer novice, it will not be necessary for you to know about the electronics of the CPU. For now, view the CPU as a magic device somewhere inside the case of your computer and don't give it another thought!

The main input device of the IBM Personal Computer is the computer keyboard. We will discuss the special features of the keyboard in Section 2.5. For now think of the keyboard as a typewriter. By typing symbols on the keyboard, you are inputting them to the computer.

The IBM Personal Computer has a number of output devices. The most basic is the "TV screen" (sometimes called the video monitor or **video**

---

* IBM Personal Computer is a registered trademark of International Business Machines Corporation.

1.2 What is a Computer?

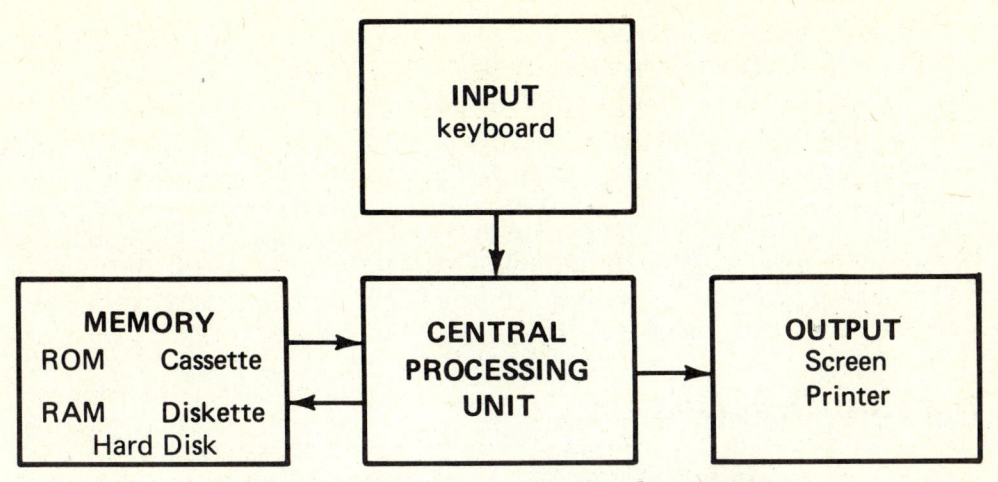

```
                    ┌──────────────┐
                    │    INPUT     │
                    │   keyboard   │
                    └──────┬───────┘
                           │
                           ▼
┌─────────────────┐  ┌──────────────┐  ┌──────────────┐
│    MEMORY       │  │   CENTRAL    │  │   OUTPUT     │
│ ROM   Cassette  │→ │  PROCESSING  │→ │   Screen     │
│ RAM   Diskette  │← │    UNIT      │  │   Printer    │
│    Hard Disk    │  │              │  │              │
└─────────────────┘  └──────────────┘  └──────────────┘
```

Figure 1-1. The main components of a computer.

display). You may also use a printer to provide output on paper. In computer jargon, printed output is called **hard copy**.

There are five types of memory in an IBM Personal Computer: **ROM**, **RAM**, **cassette**, **diskette**, and **hard disk**. Each of these types of memory has its own advantages and disadvantages. Microcomputers attempt to make memory as versatile as possible by using several kinds of memory, thereby allowing them to take advantage of the good features of each.

ROM

ROM stands for "read only memory." The computer can read ROM but cannot write anything in it. ROM is reserved for certain very important programs necessary to the operation of the machine. These programs are recorded in ROM at the factory and you may not change them.

RAM

RAM stands for "random access memory." This is the memory that you can read and write. If you type characters on the keyboard, they are then stored in RAM. Similarly, results of calculations are kept in RAM awaiting output to you. As we shall see, RAM even holds the instructions that perform the calculations!

There is an extremely important feature of RAM that you should remember:

If the computer is turned off, RAM is erased.
---

8   A First Look at Computers

Therefore, RAM may not be used to store data in permanent form. Nevertheless, it is used as the computer's main working storage, because of its great speed. (It takes about a millionth of a second to store or retrieve a piece of data from RAM.)

The size of RAM is measured in **bytes**. Essentially, a byte is a single character (such as "A" or "!"). You will often hear statements such as: "The PC/XT comes with 128K of RAM." The abbreviation "K" stands for the number 1024. And 128K stands for 128 times 1024 or 131,072 bytes.

To make permanent copies of programs and data, we may use either a cassette recorder, a diskette drive, or a hard disk.

Cassette Recorder

The cassette recorder is just a tape recorder that allows recording of information in a form the computer can understand. The recording tape is the same sort you use for musical recordings.

Diskette Drives

A diskette drive (See Figure 1-2) records information on flexible diskettes that resemble phonograph records. The diskettes are often called "floppy disks," and they can store several hundred thousand characters each! (A double-spaced typed page contains about 3,000 characters.) (See Figure 1-3.) A diskette file can provide access to information in much less time, on the average, than a cassette recorder. On the other hand, diskette drives are more costly.

Winchester Disks

A **hard disk**, also called a **Winchester disk**, stores information on a hard platter that is sealed within either the drive unit itself or a hard plastic cartridge (Figure 1-4). Winchester disks are the most costly storage

Figure 1-2. A diskette drive.

Figure 1-3. A floppy diskette.

medium for your computer. However, they allow the most rapid access to your data and can store from five million to one hundred million characters.

In this book we will assume that your system contains at least one diskette drive.

1.3 A Grand Tour of Your IBM Personal Computer

Before we turn on the computer, let's get acquainted with the various parts of the PC. (For a discussion of the PC/XT, see the end of this section.) In Figure 1-5 we have shown the three basic components: the monitor, the keyboard, and the system unit. We assume that you have followed IBM's instructions and have properly connected the various cables between these units. Note that computer cables are designed to be inserted in only one direction. Note that the end of the cable is not square but trapezoidal in shape. (See Figure 1-6.) This odd shape guarantees that the many pins plug properly into the various holes in the mating plug.

10   A First Look at Computers

Figure 1-4. A Winchester disk drive.

In turn, this guarantees that the various signals carried by the cable are directed to their proper places.

Note that we placed the monitor on top of the system unit for convenient viewing. If you wish, however, you may place your monitor beside the system unit. The choice is yours, but by all means arrange your system for comfort and convenience. You will be using your system for many hours at a time and these little convenience features will lessen eyestrain and fatigue.

The keyboard is attached to the system unit via a coiled cord, which allows you to situate the keyboard in a comfortable position. Note also the legs which tilt the keyboard at an angle with the table. This is also a "human factors" feature that is designed to minimize fatigue. We will discuss the various other features of the keyboard in Section 2.5.

Of all the basic components, the system unit is the most mysterious. So let's explore its contents. At the front of the unit are the diskette drives. Each drive has a slot in which to insert a diskette. Put your fingers in the groove in the center of the left drive and gently pull forward. (See Figure 1-7.) Note how the door lifts. This is the position of the door for diskette insertion. (More about that later.) For now, just push the door down to its original position.

In Figure 1-8 we show the rear of the system unit. Note that there are many places to plug in cables of various sizes and shapes. (Your system

1.3 A Grand Tour of Your IBM Personal Computer 11

Figure 1-5. The IBM PC.

Figure 1-6. A computer cable.

12   A First Look at Computers

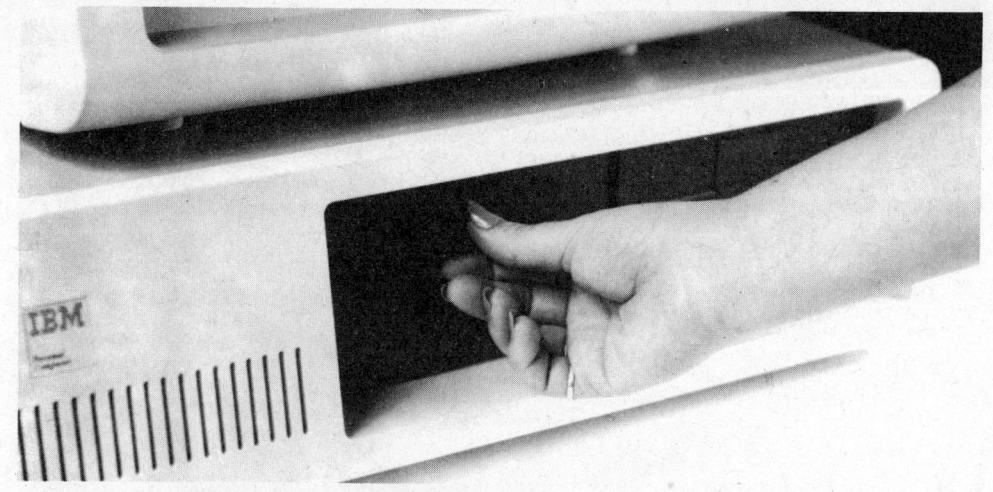

Figure 1-7. Opening the door of a diskette drive.

unit may look somewhat different, depending on the boards installed.) The system unit shown has plugs for a printer, a color display, and a communications interface. (More about each of these later.)

Figure 1-9 shows the interior of the computer. (If you are a novice, please don't remove the case of your computer; just settle for looking at the picture.) The large unit in the corner is the power source and a cooling fan. Also note the speaker in the lower left corner. The system board, which is the main electronic circuit of the computer, is situated horizontally at the bottom of the computer. The 8088 chip is on this board. The vertical boards are optional and are inserted in sockets called **expansion slots**, located on the system board. You may choose from a veritable

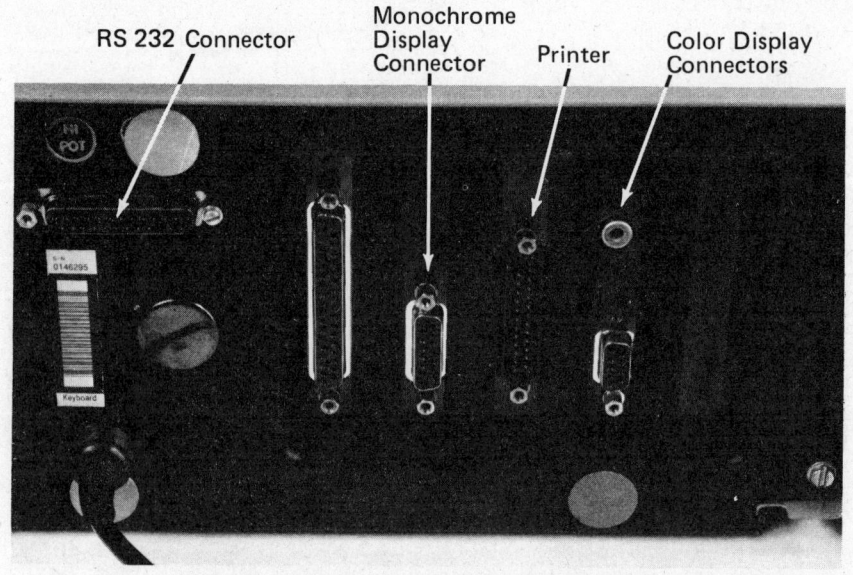

Figure 1-8. The rear of the system unit.

1.3 A Grand Tour of Your IBM Personal Computer

Figure 1-9. The interior of the IBM Personal Computer.

smorgasbord of circuit boards to expand the capabilities of your computer. The boards in Figure 1-9 are, from left to right, a monochrome display interface, a memory expansion board, a diskette controller board, and a color/graphics interface. To give you a feel for the complexity of these boards, we have shown a close-up of the color/graphics interface in Figure 1-10. In Figure 1-11, we show a close-up of a ROM chip next to a paper clip for size comparison.

Don't be intimidated by the sight of the electronic circuitry. In order to use your computer, you won't need to know how it works.

The IBM PC/XT

Figure 1-12 is a picture of the IBM PC/XT. This computer is an upgraded model of the PC. The main difference is the hard disk on the right side of the system unit instead of a second diskette drive. The hard disk system allows for as much storage as 25 diskettes used by the floppy diskette drive on its left.

1.4 Typical PC Components and Systems

In the last section we surveyed your IBM PC, both from the outside and from within. However, your system may differ quite a bit from the ones

Figure 1-10. The color/graphics interface.

shown. Indeed, the IBM PC allows (requires?) you to customize your system in very much the same way that you build a stereo system from individual components. In this section we will discuss the main component types and the various choices you have.

The typical PC system contains the following components:

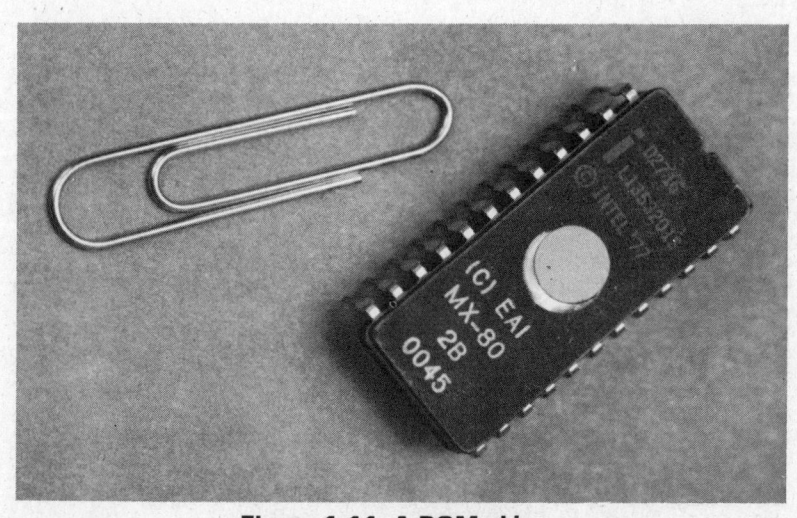

Figure 1-11. A ROM chip.

1.4 Typical PC Components and Systems 15

Figure 1-12. The IBM PC/XT.

1. System Unit
2. Keyboard
3. Disk storage
4. Monitor
5. Printer

The interconnection of these units is illustrated in Figure 1-13.

System Unit

There are two system units—the IBM PC and the IBM PC/XT. The PC/XT comes with a number of standard features that are optional on the PC. Moreover, the PC/XT has eight expansion slots compared to five for the PC.

The Keyboard

There is no choice here. All IBM PCs have the same keyboard.

16   **A First Look at Computers**

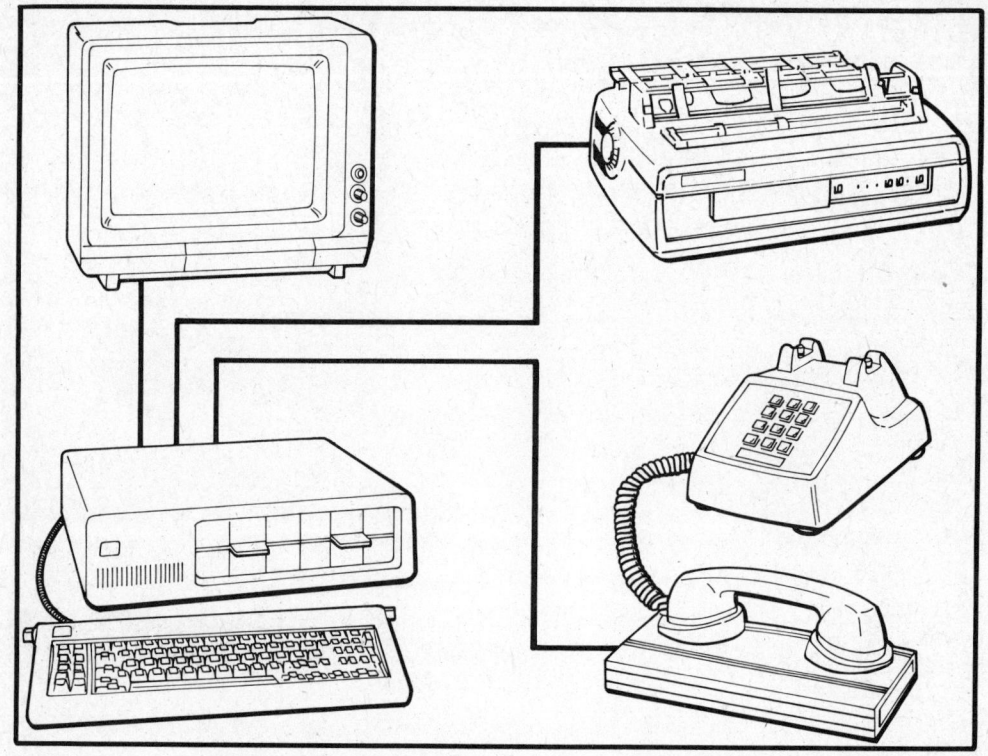

Figure 1-13. Connection of a typical PC system.

Disk Storage

You may choose among three types of disk storage:

a. Single-sided diskette drives. These drives write on only one side of a floppy diskette.
b. Double-sided diskette drives. These drives can write on both sides of a floppy diskette.
c. Winchester drives.

The PC does not come with any diskette drives as standard equipment. However, the system unit has space for either one or two such drives. The PC/XT comes with a double-sided diskette drive and a Winchester drive as standard equipment. In order to use diskette drives, you must have a diskette interface card in one of the expansion slots inside the machine. Moreover, a Winchester drive requires its own interface card.

In addition to disk storage in the system unit, you may connect additional drives in external cabinets. Such drives are connected to an appropriate interface adapter card (usually the one supplied by the drive manufacturer) in one of the expansion slots.

1.4 Typical PC Components and Systems

Monitor

You have a wide variety of monitors to choose from:

a. **The IBM Monochrome Display**—This is a "green screen" display that features exceptionally crisp letters. This display must be connected to an IBM monochrome adapter plugged into one of the expansion slots. Moreover, its power cord is plugged directly into the rear of the system unit.
b. **The IBM Color Display**—This is a color display. It must be connected to a color/graphics adapter plugged into one of the expansion slots.
c. **A home television set**—You may use your home television set as a monitor. However, you must equip the cable with a special adapter. (This is the same sort of adapter required to connect a video game to your television.)
d. **Non-IBM monitor**—All such monitors (whether color or black-and-white) must be connected to a color/graphics adapter that is plugged into one of the expansion slots.

If you use one of the monitors described in b through d, then the monitor power cord must be plugged into a power outlet (rather than the rear of the system unit).

Printer

There are two basic types of printers:

a. **Dot matrix printers**—These printers print letters as a collection of dots. They are distinguished by their speed. In this category are two IBM printers, namely:
    The IBM 80 cps Dot Matrix Printer
    The IBM Graphics Printer
b. **Daisy-wheel printers**—These printers print fully-formed letters, such as those printed by an electric typewriter. They are distinguished by the high quality of their printing, although they generally print slower than the dot matrix printers.

Your printer must be connected to the system unit. The exact nature of this connection will depend on the printer. Some printers are equipped with a **parallel interface** and some with a **serial interface**. (Don't worry about what these terms mean!) For a parallel interface you must connect the printer to a **parallel printer adapter**; for a serial interface you must connect the printer to an **asynchronous communications adapter** (also called an **RS232-C interface**).

The parallel printer adapter and the asynchronous communications adapter may each be purchased as expansion boards. However, the monochrome display adapter already includes a parallel printer adapter. Furthermore, there are many "combination" boards that include both a parallel printer adapter and an asynchronous communications adapter yet they occupy only a single expansion slot.

Other Expansion Boards

There are many other boards that you may use to expand the capabilities of your PC. Here are a few of the possibilities:

- **Game adapter**—allows your PC to use both game joysticks and a light pen.
- **Memory boards**—allow you to expand the RAM of your PC.
- **Clock/calendar**—allows your PC to keep track of the time and date, even with the machine turned off.
- **Multi-function boards**—allow various combinations of functions, such as printer adapter, game adapter, serial communications adapter, memory expansion, monochrome or color/graphics display adapter. These boards are a popular way to have many functions in your PC yet still save precious expansion slots.

Using Your PC for the First Time

2

2.1 On Diskettes and Diskette Drives

Your floppy diskette drives are a critical part of your computer system. They allow you to store and retrieve both programs and data. Before we proceed any further, let's get acquainted with these remarkable devices.

The Anatomy of a Diskette

To store information, the diskette drives use 5 ¼-inch floppy diskettes. Diskettes come in single-sided and double-sided versions. The single-sided diskettes may be written on only one side, a double-sided diskette on both sides. A single-sided diskette can accommodate approximately 163,000 characters (about 50 double-spaced typed pages), a double-sided diskette approximately twice as many.

Diskette drives come in single-sided and double-sided models. A double-sided drive can read single-sided and double-sided diskettes. However, a single-sided drive can read only single-sided diskettes.

Figure 2-1 illustrates the essential parts of a diskette. The diskette itself is a magnetically-coated circular piece of mylar plastic that rotates freely within a stiff jacket. The jacket is designed to protect the diskette. The interior of the jacket contains a lubricant that helps the diskette rotate freely within the jacket. The diskette is sealed inside. You should never attempt to open the protective jacket. The labels on the jacket identify the contents of the diskette.

The diskette drive reads and writes on the diskette through the **read-write** window. Never, under any circumstances, touch the surface of the diskette. Diskettes are very fragile. A small piece of dust or even oil from a fingerprint could damage the diskette and render parts of the information on it totally useless.

The **write protect notch** allows you to prevent changes to information on the diskette. When this notch is covered with one of the metallic labels provided with the diskettes, the computer may read the diskette, but it will not write or change any information on the diskette. To write on a diskette, the write protect notch must be uncovered.

You should have a few blank diskettes on hand. Why not take a moment to inspect one of them and locate the various parts of the diskette described above. (The labeling on your diskettes may differ from that shown in Figure 2-1.)

Cautions in Handling Diskettes

Diskettes are extremely sensitive. Here are some tips in using them.

1. Always keep a diskette in its paper envelope when it is not in use.
2. Store diskettes in a vertical position just like you would a phonograph record.

2.1 On Diskettes and Diskette Drives 21

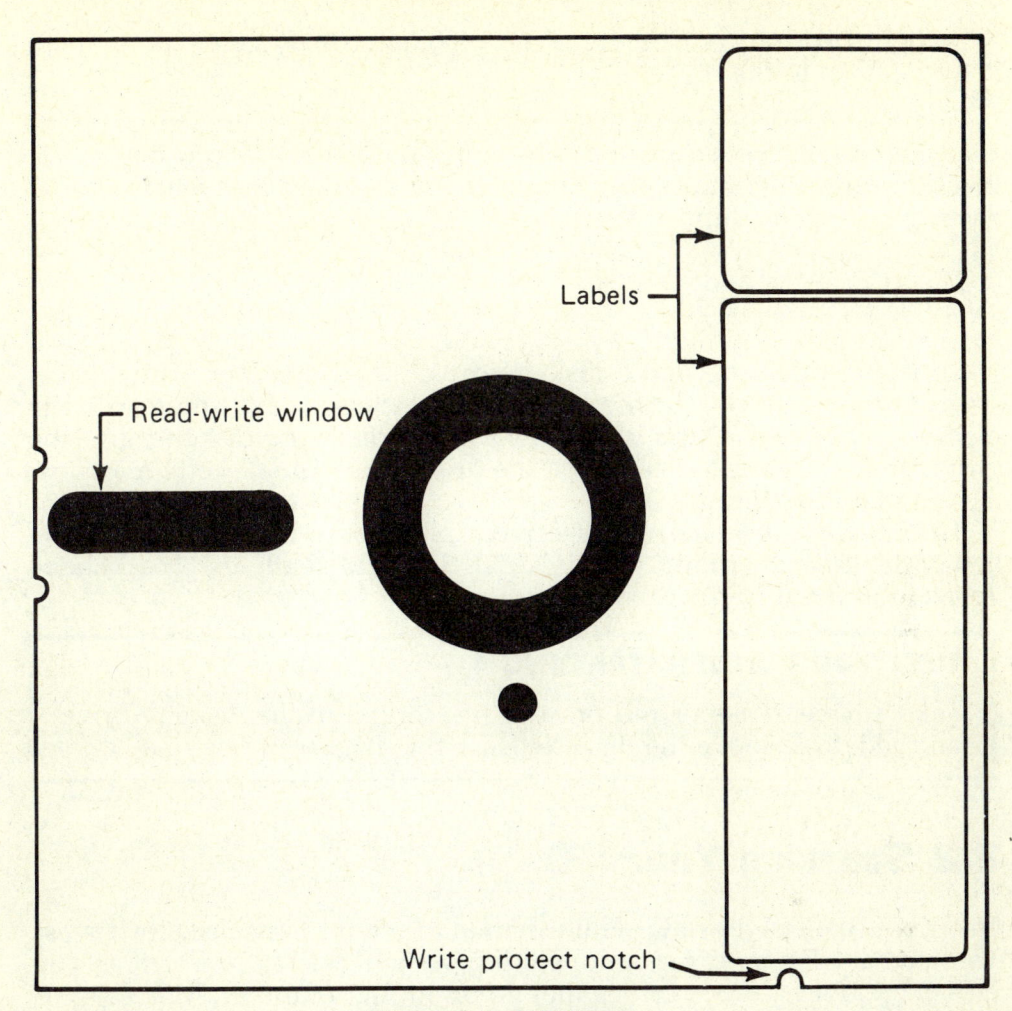

Figure 2-1. A diskette.

(Labels: Read-write window, Labels, Write protect notch)

3. Never touch the surface of a diskette or try to wipe the surface of a diskette with a rag, handkerchief, or other type of cloth.
4. Keep diskettes away from extreme heat, such as that produced by radiators, direct sun, or other sources of heat.
5. Never bend a diskette.
6. When writing on a diskette label, use only a felt-tipped pen. Never use any sort of instrument with a sharp point.
7. Keep diskettes away from magnetic fields, such as those generated by electrical motors, radios, televisions, tape recorders, telephones, and other electrical devices. A strong magnetic field may erase data on a diskette.
8. Never remove a diskette while the drive is running. (You can tell if a drive is running by the sound of the motor and the "in use"

light on the front of the drive.) Doing so may cause permanent damage to the diskette.

The above list of precautions may seem overwhelming to someone starting out. However, once you set up a suitable set of procedures for handling and storing diskettes, you will find that they are a reliable, long-lasting storage medium.

Using Diskettes

To insert a diskette into a diskette drive, open the door of the drive. Turn the diskette so that the label side is facing up and the read-write window is closest to the computer. Gently push the diskette into the drive until you hear a click. Close the drive door. The diskette may now be read by the computer.

To remove a diskette from a drive, first be sure that the light to the left of the drive door is off. Lift the drive door and gently pull the diskette forward and out of the drive.

TEST YOUR UNDERSTANDING 1

Take a blank diskette and practice inserting it in the diskette drive on the left. Remove the diskette from the drive.

2.2 Starting Your PC

In order to control the flow of information to and from the diskette drives, we need a program called an **operating system**. Such a program acts as a manager for all the activities that go on in the computer. More specifically, it coordinates the flow of information between the keyboard, video display, RAM, ROM, diskette files, and any other peripheral devices that you may have added to your computer system.

The official operating system of the IBM PC is called **IBM DOS** (IBM Disk Operating System—pronounced IBM-doss), also called **MS-DOS**, or **PC-DOS**, or just **DOS** for short. Actually, DOS has undergone several revisions since its original version. As of this moment, the latest version is DOS 2.00. We will concentrate on DOS 1.1 in this book, but our discussions also apply to DOS 2.00 with a few changes, which we will point out as we go along.

When you purchased your system, you should have also purchased a copy of a manual called **Disk Operating System** (IBM Publication 6024061 for DOS 1.1 or 6024061 for DOS 2.00). Just inside the rear cover of the DOS manual is a plastic jacket that contains a diskette labeled **DOS**.

---
*MS stands for Microsoft, the corporation that designed the operating system.

2.2 Starting Your PC

This diskette is your master copy of the programs necessary to operate your diskette drives. This diskette is extremely important. So important, in fact, that it does not have a write protect notch. This means that you can never write on this diskette. (No chance for accidentally altering its programs!) We shall refer to this diskette as the **master DOS diskette**.

In order to start your computer, it is necessary to first read DOS into the computer. Ordinarily, this would be done with a copy of the master DOS diskette rather than with the original itself. However, on your first pass through, you don't yet have any extra copies of the DOS diskette, so we must use the master. Here's the procedure to follow.

Starting Your Computer

1. Insert the DOS diskette into the diskette drive on the left (or your only diskette drive if you have only one). The label side should be up. Push the diskette to the rear of the drive until you hear a click. Close the drive door.
2. Turn on your monitor. (If you have the IBM Monochrome display, it will turn on automatically when you turn on the system unit.)
3. Turn on the printer (if one is connected).
4. On the rear of the right side of the system unit (the box where the diskette drives sit) you will find the computer On-Off switch. (See Figure 2-2.) Flick it to the up position. For about 30-45 seconds, the computer does diagnostic testing to determine if all its components are in good working order. When the tests are complete the computer should respond with a beep and the display*:

    ```
    Enter today's date (mm-dd-yy):
    ```

5. Type in today's date (in the format 4-22-99 for April 22, 1999). Press the **ENTER** key, which is the large key with the symbol:

    ↵

    The computer will respond with a display similar to:

    ```
    Enter correct time (mm:hh:ss):
    ```

    Type in the correct time. (In the format 14:03:00 for 2:03 PM. The PC uses a 24-hour clock.)
    The computer will respond with a display similar to:

    ```
    The IBM Personal Computer DOS
    Version 1.10 Copyright IBM Corp. 1981,1982
    A>_
    ```
    ↑
    (DOS prompt)

---

*Depending on your version of DOS, the displays may differ somewhat from those given above.

24 Using Your PC for the First Time

Figure 2-2.

The symbol A> is called the **DOS prompt**. It tells you that DOS is loaded and ready to accept commands.

6. In this chapter we'll learn to use many of the DOS commands. At this point let's give the command to read the BASIC programming language from the DOS diskette into RAM. Type:

```
basic
```

Press the **ENTER** key. The computer will respond with a display similar to:

```
The IBM Personal Computer Basic
Version A1.10 Copyright IBM CORP. 1981,1982
xxxxx Bytes Free
Ok  ←———————— BASIC Prompt
_   ←———————— Cursor
```

With the addition of the book's companion diskette —

You'll save time, energy (and some sanity!) when you're ready to get down to serious PC programming!

Developed by the same authors, the diskette is designed for easy use. You'll work through, modify, and examine programs at your own pace. Without the annoyance of keystroke or programming errors.

Incorporating all the programs from the text (more than **40** in all!), it includes word processing ... bar generation ... form letter generation ... list management ... computer games ... and more. It even comes complete with its own documentation!

You get all that, plus peace of mind, for only $24.95!

To order, use this handy, postage-paid envelope. Enclose a check or money order for $24.95, plus local sales tax. Or charge it to your VISA or MasterCard.

Why not do it today?

☐ **YES!** I want to make learning my PC as fast and easy as possible. Please rush me **Diskette to Accompany IBM PC: An Introduction to the Operating System, BASIC Programming and Applications - Revised and Enlarged** /D5262-3. I have enclosed payment of $24.95 plus sales tax.

Name _____

Address _____

City _____ State____ Zip_____

Charge my Credit Card Instead
☐ VISA   ☐ MasterCard

_____
Account Number

_____
Expiration Date

_____
Signature as it appears on Card

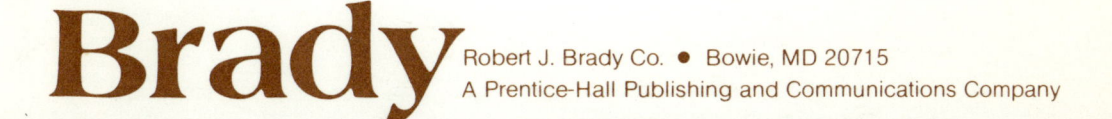

Brady
Robert J. Brady Co. • Bowie, MD 20715
A Prentice-Hall Publishing and Communications Company

Congratulations on a smart purchase!

Now — turn your book into an even more powerful learning tool!

(And eliminate hours of frustrating programming errors as well.)

See other side for details . . .

BUSINESS REPLY MAIL
FIRST CLASS PERMIT NO. 1976 BOWIE, MD

POSTAGE WILL BE PAID BY ADDRESSEE

Robert J. Brady Co.
A Prentice-Hall Company
Bowie, Maryland 20715

NO POSTAGE NECESSARY IF MAILED IN THE UNITED STATES

Note the letters **Ok** in the last line of the display. These letters are the **BASIC prompt** and indicate that the computer language (called BASIC) is ready to accept instructions. The small blinking box is called the **cursor** and indicates the place on the screen where the next typed character will appear.

7. To return from BASIC to DOS, type:

    system

    and press ENTER. The computer will display the DOS prompt A>.

TEST YOUR UNDERSTANDING 1*(answers on page 25)

a. Turn on your computer and load DOS.
b. Load BASIC.
c. Return to DOS.

Turning Off the Computer

1. Turn off the system unit.
2. Turn off the monitor. (This step is not necessary if you are using the IBM monochrome display.)
3. Remove any diskettes from the drives.

ANSWERS TO TEST YOUR UNDERSTANDING 1

1: a. Follow the instructions 1-7 for Starting Your Computer.
   b. Follow instruction 6.
   c. Follow instruction 7.

2.3 More About Diskette Drives

The IBM Personal Computer may be equipped with as many as four diskette drives. One or two may be installed in the system unit. Any others are placed in a separate cabinet, connected to the system unit by means of a cable. These are called **external drives**.

The diskette drives are given the names A:, B:, C:, D: (Note the colons). The left drive in your system unit is called A:, the right drive B:. The external drives are called C: and D:. The drive names are used to refer to a drive within a command.

At any given moment, one of your drives is designated as the **current drive**. If you give a command without mentioning the drive label, the

---

*Answers to TEST YOUR UNDERSTANDING questions (where appropriate) are given at the end of the current section in each chapter.

computer will assume that you mean the current drive. When the computer is first turned on, the current drive is set equal to A: . Another name for the current drive is the **default drive**.

The DOS prompt always indicates the current drive. If you see the prompt A>, then the current drive is A: . If you see the prompt B>, then the current drive is B: .

To change the current drive:

1. Obtain the DOS prompt A> or B> .
2. Type the name of the new current drive (remember the colon). Press ENTER.

TEST YOUR UNDERSTANDING 1 (answers on page 26)

a. Turn on your computer and change the current drive from A: to B: .
b. Change the current drive back to A: .

ANSWER TO TEST YOUR UNDERSTANDING 1

1: a. After turning on the computer and getting the DOS prompt, type B: and press ENTER.
   b. Type A: and press ENTER.

2.4 Backing Up Your DOS Diskette

Good programming practice dictates that you keep duplicate copies of all your diskettes. In computer language a copy is called a **backup**. Making backups will reduce the chance that you will lose your programs and data due to accidents (power blackout, coffee spilled on a diskette, and so forth). It is an especially good idea to make a copy of the master DOS diskette the first time you use it. Later, you should use only the copy. The original DOS diskette should be stored in a safe place so that yet another copy can be made if the first copy is damaged. Here is the procedure for making a backup copy of a diskette. (The instructions are for single drive systems. For systems with two drives, see the comment below.)

Copying One Diskette Onto Another

We must copy the contents of the master DOS diskette onto a blank diskette.

1. Obtain the DOS prompt A> . Insert the DOS diskette into drive A:. Type

   ```
   DISKCOPY
   ```

   followed by pressing the **ENTER** key. The computer will respond with the display:

   ```
   Insert source diskette in drive A
   Strike any key when ready
   ```

2. The source diskette, namely the DOS diskette, is already in drive A, so strike any key. The computer will copy a portion of DOS into RAM. When it has copied as much as it can, it will display

   ```
   Insert target diskette in drive A
   Strike any key when ready
   ```

   Remove the DOS diskette and insert a blank diskette. Next, press any key. The computer will now copy the data in RAM onto the diskette. If there is more data to be copied from the DOS diskette, you will be directed to reinsert the DOS diskette. Then steps 1 and 2 will be repeated a number of times. After all the data has been copied, the computer will display something like

   ```
   Copy complete
   Copy another? (Y/N)
   ```

   Answer N to indicate that we do not wish to copy another diskette. The computer will now display the DOS prompt:

   ```
   A>
   ```

3. Your blank diskette is now an exact copy of the original. At this point, you may give another DOS command or request BASIC.

Two-Drive Systems

To copy the contents of the diskette in A: onto the diskette in B:, proceed as above except use the command

```
DISKCOPY A: B:
```

Notice that the source drive (the one you are copying from) is listed first and the target drive (the one you are copying to) is listed second.

> **TEST YOUR UNDERSTANDING 1 (answer on page 28)**
>
> Make a copy of the DOS system diskette supplied with your diskette operating system.

If you are using DOS version 1.0 or 1.05, it is necessary to format the blank diskette prior to using the diskcopy command. (See the discussion on formatting in Chapter 3.)

From now on you should use only the **copy** of the master DOS diskette and **not** the original. Put the original in a safe place so that it may be used to make yet another copy if the current copy is damaged.

A Word to the Wise

The backup procedure just described may be used to copy the contents of any diskette onto any other. Because diskettes are fragile, it is strongly urged that you maintain duplicate copies of all your diskettes. A good procedure is to update your copies at the end of each session with the computer. This may seem like a big bother, but it will prevent untold grief if, by some mishap, a diskette with critical programs or data is erased or damaged.

TEST YOUR UNDERSTANDING 2 (answer on page 28)

Use your copy of the master DOS diskette to make another copy. (A copy of a copy is just as good as the original!)

ANSWERS TO TEST YOUR UNDERSTANDINGS 1 and 2

1: Follow instructions 1-3 on page 27.
2: Follow instructions 1-3 on page 27, except start with the copy DOS diskette in drive A:.

2.5 The Keyboard

Let us examine the PC keyboard. (See Figure 2-3.) This keyboard looks complex but can be understood if we examine it a section at a time. Let's begin with central section. (See Figure 2-4.)

The central section is very much like a typewriter keyboard. There are a few symbols which are not present on a typewriter, such as:

$<$
$>$
$\wedge$
$\sim$
$|$
$\backslash$
$\{$
$\}$

2.5 The Keyboard 29

Figure 2-3. The IBM Personal Computer keyboard.

Figure 2-4. The central section of the keyboard.

You should also note the following important differences from a typewriter keyboard:

1. There are separate keys for 1 (one) and l (el). (Many typewriters use the lower case l to do double duty as a one.)

2. The number 0 (zero) has a slash through it. This is to distinguish it from the letter o (oh).

Here are the functions of the other keys in the central portion of the keyboard:

Space bar. Generates a blank space just like the space bar on a typewriter.

Shift key. Shifts keys to their upper case meanings. For keys with two symbols, the upper symbol takes effect. The upper case meanings are in effect only as long as the shift key is held down. Releasing the shift key causes keys to assume their lower case meanings. Note that there are two shift keys, one on each side of the keyboard.

Caps Lock key. See the discussion on page 33.

Backspace key. Moves the cursor back one space. Erases any letter it backs over.

ENTER key. Similar to a carriage return key on a typewriter. Used to end a line and to place the cursor at the beginning of the next line. A line may be corrected with backspaces until ENTER is pressed.

Tab key. Works like the tab key on a typewriter. Moves the cursor to the next tab stop.

Control key. Used in combination with other keys. For example, the key combination Ctrl-A means to simultaneously press Ctrl and A. Such combinations are used to generate control codes for screen and printer.

Escape key. Used to indicate that certain sequences of letters are to be interpreted as control codes.

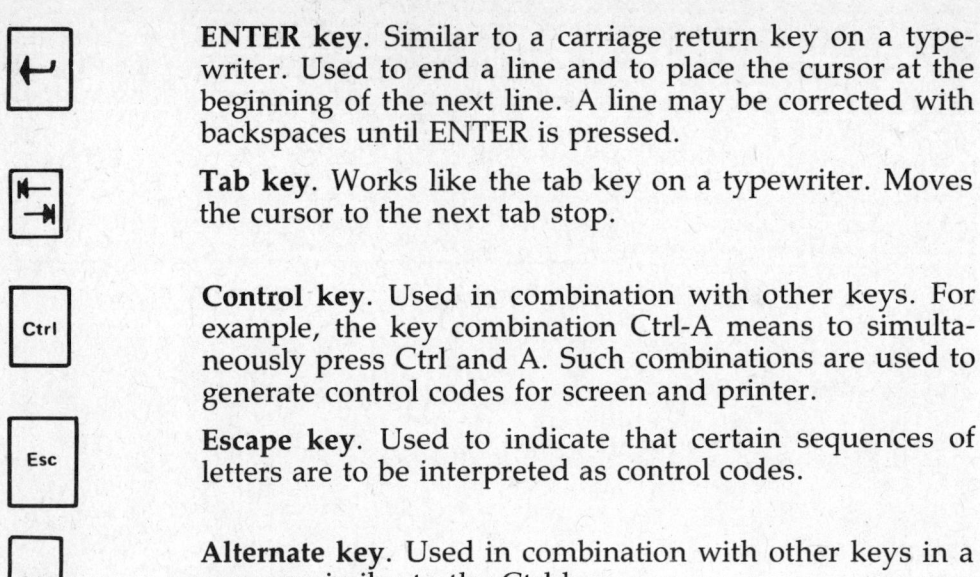

Alternate key. Used in combination with other keys in a manner similar to the Ctrl key.

PrtSc key. Use to print the screen. (See the discussion below.)

Turn on your PC and obtain the DOS prompt A>. Strike a few keys to get the feel of the keyboard. Note that as you type the corresponding characters will appear on the screen. Also note how the cursor travels along the typing line. It always sits at the location where the next typed character will appear.

As you type, you should notice the similarities between the IBM Personal Computer keyboard and that of a typewriter. However, you should also note the differences. At the end of a typewriter line you return the carriage, either manually or, on an electric typewriter, with a carriage return key. Of course, your screen has no carriage to return. However, you still must tell the computer that you are ready to move on to the next line. This is accomplished by hitting the **ENTER** key. If you press the **ENTER** key, the cursor will then return to the next line and position itself at the extreme left side of the screen. The **ENTER** key also has another function. It signals the computer to accept the line just typed. Until you hit the **ENTER** key, you may add to the line, change portions, or even erase it. (We'll learn to do these editing procedures shortly.)

Keep typing until you are at the bottom of the screen. If you hit **ENTER**, the entire contents of the screen will move up one line and the line at the top of the screen will disappear. This movement of lines on and off the screen is called **scrolling**.

As you may have already noticed, the computer will respond to some of your typed lines with error messages. Don't worry about these now.

The computer has been taught to respond only to certain typed commands. If it encounters a command that it doesn't recognize, it will announce this fact with an error message. It is extremely important for you to realize that these errors will in no way harm the computer. In fact, there is little you can do to hurt your computer (except by means of physical abuse, of course). Don't be intimidated by the occasional slaps on the wrist handed out by your computer. Whatever happens, don't let these "slaps" stop you from experimenting. The worst that can happen is that you might have to turn your computer off and start all over!

System Reset

You may restart the computer from the keyboard by pressing the **Ctrl**, **Alt**, and **Del** keys simultaneously. This key sequence will return the computer to the state it was in just after being turned on. Both RAM and the screen will be erased.

Printing the Screen

The PC provides several features that let you print what appears on the screen. Obtain the DOS prompt A> and press the key combination Ctrl-PrtSc. (Also make sure your printer is turned on.) All subsequent text that appears on your screen will also be printed. This provides you with a written record of a session at the computer. To turn off the printing, press Ctrl-PrtSc again.

You may obtain a printed copy of the current screen by pressing the key combination Shift-PrtSc. If you are in BASIC, this will work only using 2.00 or later versions.

TEST YOUR UNDERSTANDING 1 (answers on page 35)

Print the current contents of the screen.

Keyboard Usage in BASIC

Many of the keys have special meanings while BASIC is running. To illustrate this keyboard usage, let's load BASIC by obtaining the DOS prompt and typing

    basic

followed by ENTER. When you obtain the BASIC prompt, begin typing. Notice that if you neglect to end a line, it spills over onto the next. However, after almost three lines (255 characters) BASIC automatically terminates the line, just as if you had pressed ENTER.

Using Your PC for the First Time

Scrolling and corrections using the backspace key work pretty much the same in BASIC as they do in DOS.

Fill your screen with 8 or 10 lines of text. To erase the screen, use this key combination:

```
Ctrl-Home
```

All characters on the screen will be erased and only the cursor will remain. The cursor is positioned in the upper left corner of the screen, its so-called "home" position.

Numeric Keypad

Let us now turn our attention to the right side of the keyboard. Note that each of the digits 0-9 appear twice: Once in the usual place at the top of the keyboard and a second time at the right hand side. (See Figure 2-5.) The numeric keys on the right side are arranged like the keys of a calculator and are designed to make typing numbers easier. It makes no difference which set of numerical keys you use. In fact, you may alternate them in any manner, entering a 1 from the top set, then a 5 from the right set, and so forth. The right set of keys is called the **numeric keypad**.

Figure 2-5. The numeric keypad.

Actually, the keys of the numeric keypad do double duty. They are also used in BASIC for editing (for altering text that has already been typed). For now just remember that the Num Lock key controls which function the keys of the numeric keypad assume. When the **Num Lock** key is engaged, the numeric keypad functions like a calculator keyboard. With the Num Lock key disengaged, the numeric keypad is used for editing. When the computer is first turned on, the keypad is set for editing. So for your first use of the numeric keypad, it will be necessary to disengage the **Num Lock** key.

Editing Keys

Let's now describe the functions of the keys on the numeric keypad when used for editing. (The Num Lock key must be engaged.)

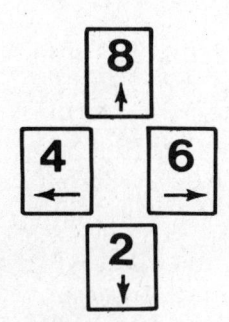

Cursor Motion Keys. These four arrow keys are used to move the cursor in the indicated directions. Note that these keys move the cursor only in BASIC. Don't confuse the up arrow with the shift key.

Insert Key. When this key is pressed, you may insert text at the current cursor position. As text is inserted, existing text is moved to the right to accommodate the new letters. The effect of the **Ins** key is canceled either by pressing Ins again, by pressing Del, by pressing ENTER, or by using the cursor motion keys.

Delete Key. When this key is pressed, one letter is deleted at the cursor position.

Use of the Caps Lock Key. In most computer work it is convenient to type using only capital letters. For one thing, capitals are larger and easier to read on the screen. You may turn off the lower case letters by depressing the **Caps Lock** key. In this mode, the letter keys are automatically typed as capitals. *Note, however, that the non-letter keys (such as 1 and !) still have two meanings. To type the upper symbol, you must still use the* **SHIFT** *key*. To exit from the all-capitals mode, once again press the **Caps Lock** key. With the Caps Lock key engaged, if you press the shift key and a letter key, a lower case letter will be displayed.

TEST YOUR UNDERSTANDING 2 (answers on page 35)
a. Type your name on the screen.
b. Erase the screen.
c. Repeat a. using all capital letters. (Don't worry about the computer's response to your typing!)

Line Width. The IBM Personal Computer allows lines to contain either 40 characters or 80 characters per line. To switch from one line width to the other, we use the WIDTH command. To switch to 40 characters per line type

```
WIDTH 40
```

followed by ENTER. To return to 80 characters per line, type

```
WIDTH 80
```

followed by ENTER. In the rest of this text, we will assume that the lines are 80 characters wide. If you use a 40-character line width, your displays may look somewhat different from those indicated.

Note that if you are using the IBM Monochrome Display, then the WIDTH 40 command will cause the characters to be displayed 40 across, only on the left half of the screen.

Function Key Display. Note that the last line of the screen is filled with data that does not change as you type. This data displays the assignment of certain user-programmable keys, F1-F10 at the left side of the keyboard. (See Figure 2-6.) If your screen is set to display a 40-character wide display, then only the definitions of keys F1-F5 are displayed. The function keys F1-F10 may be programmed to generate certain often-used key sequences or words. Figure 2-7 shows the initial function key display. You may turn off the function key display by typing

```
KEY OFF
```

followed by **ENTER**. If you wish to turn on the display, type

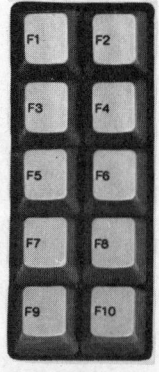

Figure 2-6. Function Keys.

KEY ON

By keeping the display line off you make the last screen line available for program use.

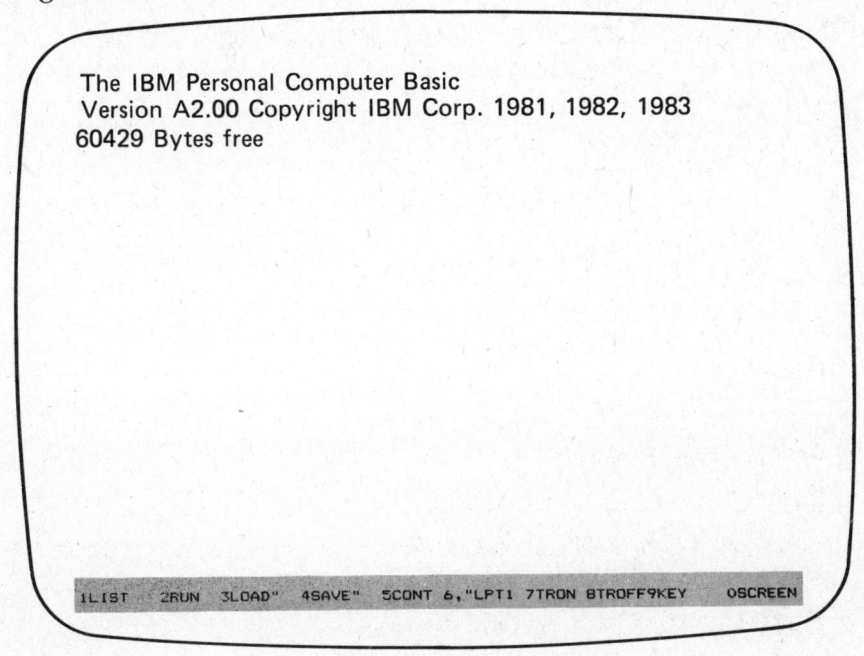

```
The IBM Personal Computer Basic
Version A2.00 Copyright IBM Corp. 1981, 1982, 1983
60429 Bytes free




















1LIST  2RUN  3LOAD"  4SAVE"  5CONT 6,"LPT1 7TRON 8TROFF9KEY    0SCREEN
```

Figure 2-7. Function key display.

Exercises

Type the following expressions on the screen. After each numbered exercise clear the screen. (These exercises contain some typical expressions you will be typing when you use BASIC. They are provided as practice in typing and in manipulating the keyboard.)

1. 10 Print "Hello."
2. 10 ARITH1 = 1.5378
3. 10 PRINT 3+7
4. 20 LET A = 3−5
5. 20 5% of 68
6. 10 IF 38 > −5
7. 10 X=5: PRINT X
8. 20 IF X>0 THEN 50
9. 10 LET X=0
   20 LET Y=50.35
10. 200 Y = X*2 − 5
    300 PRINT Y,"Y"

ANSWERS TO TEST YOUR UNDERSTANDINGS 1 and 2

1: Press Shift-PrtSc simultaneously.
2: a. Type your name, ending the line with ENTER.
   b. Hit Ctrl and Home simultaneously.
   c. Hit Caps Lock. Now repeat part a.

An Introduction to DOS

3

38 An Introduction to DOS

DOS intrudes into every aspect of PC use. It is no exaggeration to say that every time you sit down at your computer, you are using DOS. In this chapter we will learn to use some of the most essential DOS commands.

3.1 Files and File Names

The contents of a diskette are broken into units called **files**. For our present purposes you may think of a file as a collection of characters. For example, the characters comprising Section 3.1 of this book, when stored on diskette, might comprise one file. (In fact, as this book was being written, the sections were stored on diskette in exactly that way.)

A diskette may contain many files. (The maximum number depends on which version of DOS you are using as well as on the type of drives your computer has.) However, diskette files may be classified into two broad categories—programs and data files.

Programs. A program is a sequence of computer instructions. Throughout this book we will be discussing programs of one sort or another—programs to compute loan interest, to play Tic Tac Toe, and to print form letters, to mention but a few.

Data files. A data file contains data, such as payroll information, personnel data, recipes, train and airline schedules, appointment calendars, and so forth. Programs often make use of data files. This is done by including instructions within the program for reading (or writing) on particular data files. In this way you may, for example, look up appointments and let the computer make decisions based on data in the file.

File Names

Each file is identified by a **file name**. Here are some examples of valid file names:

BASIC.COM
FORMAT.COM
PAYROLL
GAME.001

A file name consists of two parts—the main file name (BASIC,FORMAT,PAYROLL,GAME) and an optional extension (COM,COM, no extension, 001). The main file name may contain as many as eight characters, the extension as many as three. The two parts of the file name are separated by a period.

The following characters are allowed in a file name:

The letters A-Z
The digits 0-9
Any of these characters:
! @ # $ % & ( ) - _ { } ' `

Note that a file name cannot include any of the following characters:

¦ \ < > , / ? " ~ : + = * ^

The only period allowed in a file name is the one that separates the two parts of the file name. Moreover, a file name cannot have any spaces.

A file name may be spelled with either upper or lower case letters. However, DOS will convert the file name into upper case. So, for example, the file names

JOHN   John

refer to the same file.

> **TEST YOUR UNDERSTANDING 1 (answers on page 40)**
> What is wrong with the following file names?
> a. ALICE 01   b. #2324/1   c. alphabetical

A particular diskette can have only one file with a particular name. However, there is nothing to stop you from using the same file name to refer to different files on **different** diskettes.

When you name a file, choose a name which somehow suggests the contents. For example, if you generate a monthly payroll file, you may name the various monthly files:

PAYROLL.JAN, PAYROLL.FEB, PAYROLL.MAR,...

and so forth.

The Directory

Each diskette has a directory that lists the name of each file on the diskette as well as some descriptive information about the file. Let's analyze one directory entry, the one for the file named DISKCOPY.COM. Actually this file is a program, and one that we've already used, namely the program for copying the contents of one diskette onto another. We used this program to backup our master DOS diskette. The directory entry for DISKCOPY.COM reads*

```
DISKCOPY   COM    2444   3-08-83   12:00p
```

The first two parts of the entry, namely DISKCOPY and COM, give the file name and the extension. The next part of the entry gives the size of the file in bytes. DISKCOPY.COM is 2444 bytes long. The final two parts of the directory entry give the date and time the file was last changed. In this example, DISKCOPY.COM was last altered on 3-08-83 at 12:00PM.

---

*This display corresponds to DOS 2.00. DOS 1.1 is 2008 bytes and was created 5-07-82 at 12:00p.

DOS maintains the directory automatically. Each time a file is added or changed, DOS makes the appropriate changes in the directory so that it accurately reflects the contents of the diskette.

You may examine the directory of a diskette using the DOS command DIR. For example, to examine the directory of the diskette in drive A:, you would type

DIR A:

and press ENTER. The directory of drive A: will then be displayed on the screen.

To display the directory of the diskette in drive B:, you would use the command

DIR B:

If you wish to display the directory of the current drive, you may omit the drive name. That is, the command

DIR

displays the directory of the diskette in the current drive.

TEST YOUR UNDERSTANDING 2 (answer on page 40)

Display the directory of your DOS diskette.

TEST YOUR UNDERSTANDING 3 (answer on page 40)

Suppose that a diskette contains too many files to be displayed on the screen at one time. How can you determine the entire directory?

Exercises (answers on page 366)

Which of the following file names are valid? If invalid, tell why.

1. SALLY.001
2. EXAMPLE.TXT
3. E>
4. S:001
5. #$%&{}
6. A.B.C
7. ACCOUNT.0123
8. DEMONSTRATION.823

ANSWERS TO TEST YOUR UNDERSTANDINGS 1, 2, and 3

1: a. Illegal space
   b. Illegal character (/)
   c. Too many characters
2: Place the DOS diskette in the current drive, type:
   DIR
   and press ENTER.

> 3: Use Ctrl-PrtSc to print the contents of the screen as they are displayed.

3.2 File Specifications

As we mentioned in the preceding section, two different files may have the same name as long as they are on separate diskettes. But what happens when you put one of the diskettes in drive A: and one in drive B:? Clearly, there is potential for dangerous confusion here. In order to specify a file without ambiguity, you must give, in addition to the file name, the location of the file.

PC Device Names

DOS specifies the various components of the PC using the following abbreviations:

A:, B:, C:, D: disk drives
    (diskette drives or hard disks)
CON: the console (or keyboard)
SCRN: the screen
LPT1: printer #1
LPT2: printer #2
COM1: communications adapter #1
COM2: communications adapter #2

(Most systems will have only one printer and one communications adapter attached. However, DOS allows for expansion.)

File Specifications

The combination of a device name and a file name is called a **file specification**. Here are some examples:

A:ACCOUNTING
COM1:XYZ.01
LPT1:PRINT.2

Each file has an associated file specification that tells the location of the file and the file name. The file specification contains enough information to find the file without any ambiguities.

In order for a file specification to be valid, both the device name and the file name must be valid.

You may omit the device name from a file specification. In this case, DOS will assume that the device is the current diskette drive. For example, suppose that the current drive is B:. Then the file specification ARITH.ADD is understood to stand for

```
B:ARITH.ADD
```

Wild Card Characters

The characters * and ? in a file name have a special meaning for DOS.
The character * may be used as either the main file name or the extension. The portion of the file name replaced by * may be anything at all. For example, consider this file name:

```
*.COM
```

This file name stands for any file with the extension COM. Similarly, the file name

```
WS.*
```

stands for any file that has as its main name WS. Finally, the file name

```
*.*
```

stands for any file.

Such "ambiguous" file names can shorten various DOS commands. For example, we may copy a file from one diskette to another using the COPY command. (See Section 4.) To copy all files from the diskette in drive A: to the diskette in drive B:, we give the simple command

```
COPY A:*.* B:
```

Similarly, to copy all files on the diskette in drive A: and having an extension COM onto the diskette in drive B:, we use the command

```
COPY A:*.COM B:
```

The character ? in a file name allows a single character to be ambiguous. For example, consider this file name:

```
EXAMPLE.00?
```

The third letter in the extension may be anything. Similarly, consider this file name:

```
NIG??.000
```

The main file name has five letters, begins with NIG, and the last two letters of the main file name may be anything.

File names using * and ? may be used in file specifications.

Exercises (answers on page 366)

Write file specifications for the following files:

1. ALICE.3 on COM1:
2. MESSAGE on LPT1:

3. Any file on the diskette in drive A:.
4. Any file on the current drive.
5. A file on drive A: in which the main file name has only one letter.
6. A file on drive A: in which the main file name is RALPH and the extension may be anything.

3.3 Executing Commands and Programs

DOS has many commands that perform "housekeeping" functions for the PC. For example, we have already met the command DISKCOPY which allows you to copy the contents of one diskette onto another, and the command DIR that allows you to display a diskette directory. In the remainder of this chapter we will discuss the various DOS commands and how to use them. However, let's first make some general comments about DOS commands.

In order to execute a DOS command, the DOS prompt must be displayed. Then do the following:

1. Type the DOS command.
2. Press ENTER.

DOS will execute the command. When execution is complete, DOS will redisplay the DOS prompt.

We have already met the above procedure in our discussions of the DOS commands DIR and DISKCOPY.

Before you press ENTER, you may use the BACKSPACE key to correct mistakes. If you make an error in a command, DOS is quite tolerant. For example, give the command XXXXXX. (There is no such command.) DOS will respond with:

```
Bad Command or File Name
A>
```

You may now give another command.

Before you press ENTER, you may press the **Esc** key. This erases the current line and allows you to retype the command.

Here's another type of error that can occur. Remove the DOS diskette and type the command DISKCOPY A: B:. DOS will attempt to read the DISKCOPY program from the non-existent diskette. After a few seconds, DOS will respond with the prompt

```
Error reading drive A:
Repeat(R), Ignore(I), or Abort(A)
```

Type R to repeat the command (presumably after you have replaced the diskette), I to ignore the error (in this case, you will generate the same error message), or A (in which case the command will be canceled and the DOS prompt redisplayed). Note that in typing R, I, or A, you don't need to type ENTER.

Internal vs External DOS Commands

We have already noted that the command DISKCOPY is contained in the file DISKCOPY.COM on the DOS diskette. However, if you inspect the directory of the DOS diskette, you will not find a file named anything like DIR.COM . So where does DOS obtain the program corresponding to the command DIR ? The answer lies in the way DOS works.

When you start your computer system, you read part of DOS into RAM. This portion of DOS stays in RAM throughout your session with the computer. The most important DOS commands are contained in this portion of DOS so that they can be available without fetching them from diskette. Such commands are called **internal commands** and DIR is an example. You may remove the DOS diskette from the current drive and still have the internal DOS commands available.

It would be nice to have all of DOS' commands in RAM all the time. For one thing, they would execute more quickly. However, this gain must be balanced against the permanent decrease in the amount of RAM. Any decrease in RAM would lower the allowable size of application programs. So, as a compromise, the least frequently used DOS commands are stored on diskette. These commands are called **external commands**. When you request an external command, the corresponding diskette file is read into memory and is executed. Upon completion, the memory is made available for the next program or command.

TEST YOUR UNDERSTANDING 1 (answer on page 45)

Remove the DOS diskette from drive A: . Give the command

```
DISKCOPY A: B:
```

What happens? Why?

Running Programs Under DOS

We have described the procedure for executing DOS commands. The same procedure may be used for programs. Many programs you purchase will be stored in files with the extensions COM or EXE. To run such a program, just type the file name without the extension and press ENTER. For example, the BASIC language is one of the programs on the DOS diskette and its file name is BASIC.COM. To run BASIC, we type BASIC and press ENTER.

Programs on Diskettes in Other Drives

So far, we have restricted our discussion to programs or commands contained on the diskette in the current drive. However, you may run a program or execute a command located anywhere. Just precede the command name by the drive designation. For example, suppose that BASIC is on the diskette in drive B:. To run this program, type

    B:BASIC

and press ENTER.

> **ANSWER TO TEST YOUR UNDERSTANDING 1**
>
> 1: DOS reports an error reading drive A: since it cannot find the file DISKCOPY.COM to read.

3.4 The COPY Command

You may move a file from one place to another within the computer using the COPY command. As you might guess, this command is very important. Here is how to use it.

1. Obtain the DOS prompt A>. (If you are in BASIC, type SYSTEM and press ENTER to obtain this prompt.)
2. To copy file specification <filespec1> to file specification <filespec2>, type

    COPY <filespec1> <filespec2>

   and press ENTER. (Note that there is a space between the two file specifications.)

For example, to copy A:BASIC.COM (this is the copy of the BASIC language BASIC.COM located on the diskette in drive A:) to drive B:, just type

    COPY A:BASIC.COM B:BASIC.COM

and press ENTER. The computer will make a copy of BASIC.COM on the diskette in drive B:.

Actually, if you wish to leave the file name the same in the copy, you may include only the device name in the second file specification. For example, the above copying operation could also be accomplished by typing

    COPY A:BASIC.COM B:

followed by ENTER.

Creating a Diskette File

We may use the COPY command to copy from the keyboard (device name CON:) directly to a diskette file. Here's how. Sit down at your computer and obtain the DOS prompt A>. Type

46 An Introduction to DOS

```
COPY CON: A:TEST
```

and press ENTER.

We have just told DOS that we wish to copy a file from the console (keyboard) to drive A: and give the resulting file the name TEST. Now type

```
This is a test.
We are creating the file TEST on drive A:.
```

End each line with ENTER. Note that the above lines are displayed on the screen. Moreover, DOS temporarily stores input lines in RAM. To indicate that we are done inputting data, press function key F6 followed by ENTER. DOS will now copy the input lines from RAM to a diskette file as you requested. You will see the drive light on drive A: go on. This means that the writing operation is in progress. The computer will finally respond with the message

```
1 File(s) copied
```

You have just created the file TEST. If you are not convinced, list the directory of drive A: by typing

```
DIR A:
```

followed by ENTER. Among the data appearing on the screen will be a line in this form:

```
TEST    62   2-25-83   11:15a
```

This **directory entry** tells you that the name of the file is TEST, and that it contains 62 bytes (62 characters, counting spaces, ENTERs, and so forth). The file was created on 2/25/83 at 11:15AM. (The computer will compute the date and time from the data you specified when you turned the computer on.)

If you are still not convinced that you have created a file, let's copy the file back to the screen. Type

```
COPY TEST CON:
```

and press ENTER. We have just requested that DOS copy TEST from the current drive (A:) to the console. (To the computer's way of thinking, the console consists of both the keyboard and screen.) Note that the contents of the file will be displayed on the screen.

Finally, let's copy the file TEST to the printer with the command

```
COPY TEST LPT1:
```

followed by ENTER. (Before giving the command, check to make sure that the printer is on.) The printer will print the contents of the file.

TEST YOUR UNDERSTANDING 1 (answer on page 47)

Create a file TEST2 on drive B: containing the following data:

```
This line is part of TEST2 on drive B:
```

3.4 The COPY Command

> **TEST YOUR UNDERSTANDING 2 (answer on page 47)**
>
> Redisplay TEST2 on the screen.

Using Wild Card Characters with COPY

The wild card characters ? and * are very useful in describing COPY operations. Recall that the character * replaces any sequence of characters within a main file name or an extension. For example, the file name *.001 refers to all files with an extension of 001. Some examples of file names that qualify are:

```
JANE.001    HOWARD.001    MONEY.001    A.001
```

A command of the form

```
COPY A:*.001 B:
```

will copy all files on A: with extension 001 onto B:.

To copy all the files on A: to B:, you may use this command:

```
COPY A:*.* B:
```

Recall that the wild card character ? stands for a single character. For example, the file name ??ME.001 can stand for the file names FAME.001 and NAME.001, as well as LAME.001 .

> **TEST YOUR UNDERSTANDING 3 (answer on page 47)**
>
> Write a command that copies all files on B: with an extension BAS to A:.

Exercises (answers on page 366)

Write DOS commands to:

1. Print B:TEST .
2. Copy all files with the extension COM from A: to B: .
3. Display A:TEST.
4. Copy A:TEST to B: with the new name TEST3 .
5. Copy all files from A: to B: whose file names begin with a D where the main file name has eight characters.

> **ANSWERS TO TEST YOUR UNDERSTANDINGS 1, 2, and 3**
>
> 1: Obtain the DOS prompt A>. Type the line followed by ENTER. Press F6 followed by ENTER.
> 2: Obtain the DOS prompt. Type COPY B:TEST2 CON:.
> 3: COPY B:*.BAS A:

3.5 COPYing and FORMATting Diskettes

In Chapter 2 we made several copies of the DOS master diskette. However, this diskette, important as it is, is not the only diskette we will need. Indeed, the DOS diskette has very little unused space. We need a diskette with plenty of room for use to write our own programs and data files. In this section we will learn to prepare such diskettes.

Formatting a Diskette

When DOS writes on a diskette, it does so in a very orderly fashion. Data is written in circular rings called **tracks**. (See Figure 3-1.) Each track is divided into a number of sectors (eight or nine depending on your version of DOS). (See Figure 3-2.)

In order for DOS to write on a diskette, the track and sector boundaries must be written on the diskette. The IBM PC uses **soft-sectored diskettes**, which means that the tracks and sector boundaries are not pre-recorded at the factory. Rather, it is your job to prepare a diskette for use by first writing these boundaries on it. This task is called **formatting** and is carried out by the DOS command FORMAT.

The FORMAT command is an external command. To use it you must start with a DOS diskette in the current drive. Type

```
FORMAT <drive>
```

Figure 3-1. The tracks of a diskette.

3.5 COPYing and FORMATing Diskettes 49

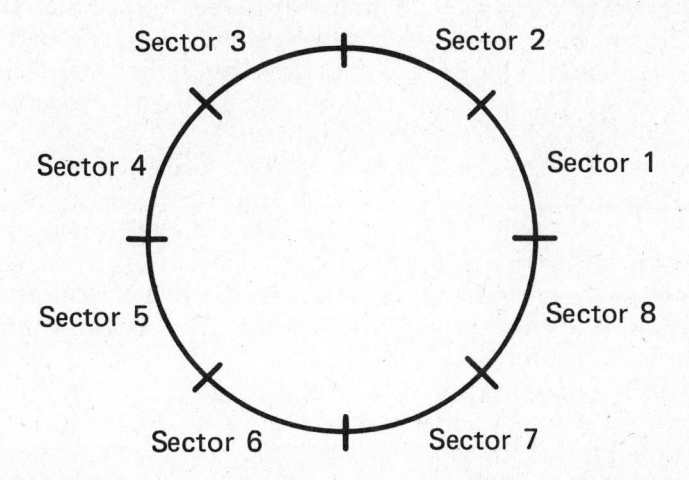

Figure 3-2. The sectors of a diskette track.

Here <drive> is the name of the drive which will contain the diskette to be formatted. For example, to format a diskette in drive A:, you would type:

```
FORMAT A:
```

DOS will respond with the prompt

```
Insert new diskette for drive A:
and strike any key when ready
```

Place a blank diskette into drive A:. (If the DOS diskette is in drive A:, don't worry about removing it. The FORMAT program is already in RAM at this point.) Press any key. The computer will proceed to format the diskette. Eventually, the display will look something like this (this display is correct for a single-sided drive):

```
Formatting...Format Complete
160,256 bytes on diskette
160,256 bytes available
Format another (Y/N)?
```

At this point you may answer the question Y(=YES) and format another diskette or N(=NO), in which case DOS will terminate the FORMAT operation and redisplay the DOS prompt, awaiting your next command.

The above procedure has been designed so that you may format diskettes one after another. It's a good idea to format an entire box of diskettes when you first buy it. By doing this, you know that all the blank diskettes you have lying around are ready for writing.

The numbers displayed in your final FORMAT prompt may be different from those above. First of all, the number of bytes on a diskette depends on the type of diskette drive (one-sided or two-sided). It also depends on which version of DOS you are using. DOS 2.00 can record nine sectors per track, whereas DOS 1.1 records eight.

If you are using DOS 1.1 or 2.00 in a two-sided drive, the FORMAT command will automatically format your diskette as a two-sided diskette. If the drive is one-sided, then the formatted diskette will also be one-sided. If, however, you are formatting a diskette on a two-sided drive but wish to subsequently use it on a one-sided drive, you must instruct DOS to format the diskette as single-sided. This is done using the /1 option. For example, to format the diskette in drive A: as a single-sided diskette, use the command

```
FORMAT A: /1
```

NOTE: You may reformat a diskette that has already been formatted. This erases all data on the diskette. (This is a sure way of destroying sensitive information you don't want lying around.)

TEST YOUR UNDERSTANDING 1

Format a blank diskette.

The number of bytes available will usually be the same as the number of bytes on the diskette. Occasionally, a diskette will contain microscopic flaws which prevent DOS from formatting some sectors. DOS hides these sectors in an invisible file called BADTRACK. You never need to worry about these sectors being used in one of your files and ruining your data! However, if any sectors are placed in BADTRACK, the number of bytes available on the diskette is reduced.

The diskettes produced by the above procedure are totally blank. In particular, they do not contain the DOS files necessary to start the computer. You may include the DOS internal commands on the formatted diskette by using this command:

```
FORMAT A: /S
```

A diskette produced by this command may be used to start the computer. The DOS internal commands occupy a rather small portion of the diskette. Therefore, most of the diskette is available for your use. When you format a diskette with the /S option, the final display looks something like this:

```
Formatting...Format Complete
160256 bytes on diskette
 39936 bytes used by system
120320 bytes available
Format another (Y/N)?
```

3.5 COPYing and FORMATing Diskettes

> **TEST YOUR UNDERSTANDING 2 (answers on page 51)**
>
> Format a blank diskette with the /S option.
>   a. Use this diskette to restart the computer.
>   b. Display the directory of A:. Can you explain what you see?

In Chapter 2, we learned to copy a diskette using the DISKCOPY command. We used this command to make a copy of the master DOS diskette. However, we made no mention of FORMATting in that discussion. The reason is that the DISKCOPY command automatically formats the diskette onto which it is copying (the **target diskette**). This formatting is performed only if necessary.

> **ANSWERS TO TEST YOUR UNDERSTANDING 2**
>
> 2: a. Place the formatted diskette in drive A: and press Crtl-Alt-Del simultaneously.
>   b. The only file in the directory is COMMAND.COM, which occupies 17,664 bytes (in DOS 2.00). The system occupies 39,936 bytes. The remaining bytes are contained in the main DOS files, called IBMBIOS.COM and IBMDOS.COM, which are invisible as far as the directory is concerned.

3.6 Other DOS Internal Commands

In this section we give you a brief survey of the most commonly used DOS internal commands. Remember that these commands may be used whenever the DOS prompt is displayed. They do not require any information from the DOS diskette.

ERASE allows you to erase a file. For example, to erase the file EXAMPLE.TXT on the diskette in drive A:, you could use the command

    ERASE A:EXAMPLE.TXT

If the drive designation is omitted, then the current drive is assumed. For example,

    ERASE EXAMPLE.TXT

will erase EXAMPLE.TXT on the diskette in the current drive. The erase command may be used with the wild card characters * and ?. For example, to erase all files on the diskette in drive A:, use the command

    ERASE A:*.*

52 An Introduction to DOS

> **TEST YOUR UNDERSTANDING 1 (answer on page 53)**
>
> Write a command that erases all files on the current drive with a five-character main name and an extension of COM.

RENAME allows you to rename a file. For example, to rename A:OLDFILE with the name NEWFILE, you could use the command

```
RENAME A:OLDFILE NEWFILE
```

Note that the current file name comes first and then the new file name. If you do not give a file designation with the current drive name, then the current drive is assumed.

> **TEST YOUR UNDERSTANDING 2 (answer on page 53)**
>
> Write a command that renames A:TEST.COM to A:T.COM .

DATE allows you to set the date. For example, to set the date to 4-12-83, you could use the command

```
DATE 4-12-83
```

> **TEST YOUR UNDERSTANDING 3 (answer on page 53)**
>
> Write a command that sets the date to Dec. 12, 1984.

TIME allows you to set the time. For example, to set the time to 1:04:00 PM, you could use the command

```
TIME 13:04:00
```

> **TEST YOUR UNDERSTANDING 4 (answer on page 53)**
>
> Write a command to set the time to 12:00:00 AM.

TYPE allows you to display the contents of a file. For example, to display the contents of the file A:TEST1, you could use the command

```
TYPE A:TEST1
```

If you try to display a program, it will usually look like a bunch of gibberish. Program files are designed for the convenience of the computer, not for humans. However, a text file will be displayed in readable form.

To obtain a written copy of a file, you may first press Ctrl-PrtSc. Then give the type command. The file will be displayed on the screen and also printed on your printer.

COMP allows you to compare two files to determine whether they are identical. For example, suppose that we wish to compare FILE1 on the diskette in drive A: with FILE2 on the diskette in drive B:. Give the command

```
COMP A:FILE1 B:FILE2
```

This command may be used to check on the results of a COPY operation to determine whether the copy is identical to the original. Note that the COMP command does not give you a chance to change diskettes. Therefore, the diskettes with the files needed for comparison must be in the diskettes prior to giving the COMP command.

ANSWERS TO TEST YOUR UNDERSTANDINGS 1, 2, 3, and 4

1: ERASE ?????.COM
2: RENAME A:TEST.COM A:T.COM
3: DATE 12-12-84
4: TIME 00:00:00

3.7 Other DOS External Commands

In this section we summarize some of the most commonly used DOS external commands. Note that in order to use any of these commands DOS must obtain the appropriate program from the DOS diskette.

DISKCOMP allows you to compare the contents of two diskettes, byte by byte. For example, to compare the diskettes in drives A: and B:, you could use the command

```
DISKCOMP A: B:
```

If your system has only one drive, you would also use this command for diskette comparison, even though you don't have a drive B:. DOS will prompt you to swap the diskettes in your single drive so that a comparison may be made.

CHKDSK allows you to check on the number of bytes remaining on a diskette. It also performs a check to determine if any inconsistencies exist in the way the files are stored. To perform a CHKDSK operation on the diskette in drive B:, you could use the command

```
CHKDSK B:
```

The result of this command is a display of the form

```
160256 bytes total disk space
 22272 bytes in 2 hidden files
 45455 in 4 user files
 92529 bytes available on disk

 65536 bytes total memory
 52785 bytes free
```

As usual, your numbers may vary, depending on your system, version of DOS, and so forth.

You should execute a CHKDSK every so often for each of your diskettes to assure the integrity of your files and to determine the space remaining on the diskette.

54   An Introduction to DOS

> **TEST YOUR UNDERSTANDING 1 (answer on page 54)**
>
> Suppose that the DOS diskette is in drive B: and that drive A: is the current drive. Write a command for performing CHKDSK on the diskette in drive A:.

> **ANSWER TO TEST YOUR UNDERSTANDING 1**
>
> 1: B:CHKDSK A:

3.8 Creating Your Own DOS Commands— Batch Files

In the preceding sections, we learned about the most useful DOS commands. Most often, you will execute DOS commands by typing them directly from the keyboard, as described earlier in the chapter. In many applications it is necessary to execute the same sequence of DOS commands repeatedly. For example, consider the following situation.

Suppose that you have a diskette containing four files, named ACCOUNTS.MAY, PROFIT.MAY, PAYABLE.MAY, and SALES.MAY. Your business is computerized and every one of your 10 managers has an IBM PC. Rather than distribute the contents of the files via paper copies, in the traditional manner, you wish to send each manager a copy of the files on diskette.

A simple solution would be to use DISKCOPY to make 10 copies of the diskette containing the files. Suppose, however, that your diskette also contains some sensitive information that you do not wish to circulate. In this case, you may prepare the duplicate diskettes by copying the files one at a time. This may be done via the COPY command. Here are the DOS commands required to prepare one duplicate diskette, starting from an unformatted diskette.

```
FORMAT B: /S
COPY A:ACCOUNTS.MAY B:
COPY A:PROFIT.MAY B:
COPY A:PAYABLE.MAY B:
COPY A:SALES.MAY B:
```

Assume that your files are contained on the same diskette as FORMAT.COM and that this diskette is in drive A:. The duplicate diskette is in drive B:.

It is possible to prepare the 10 duplicates by typing these commands in manually. But what a chore! It is also easy to make a mistake in typing, especially as the afternoon draws to a close. There is, fortunately, a much better way to proceed, namely to use a batch file.

3.8 Creating Your Own DOS Commands—Batch Files

A **batch file** is a diskette file consisting of a list of DOS commands. A batch file must have a file name with the extension BAT. In our case, let's name the batch file C.BAT, and let's store it on the diskette in drive A:. In order to create the batch file, use the COPY command. Type

```
COPY CON: A:C.BAT
```

and press ENTER. Now type in the DOS commands, exactly as they appear in the above list. At the end of each line, press ENTER. After the last line and its ENTER, press function key F6 and then ENTER. DOS will then respond with the message

```
1 file(s) copied
```

The file C.BAT is now on the diskette in drive A:.

In order to execute the list of DOS commands, we now merely type the letter C and press ENTER. (It is just as if we created a new DOS command with the name C.) DOS will then search the current diskette (A:), find the batch file, and execute the various commands in the order specified.

> **TEST YOUR UNDERSTANDING 1 (answer on page 57)**
>
> Modify the above list of DOS commands so that they check to make sure that the copies of the files are identical to the originals.

Now our copying job is cut down to size:

1. Insert a blank diskette into drive B:.
2. Type C and press ENTER.
3. Wait for the commands to be executed.
4. Repeat operations 1-3 until all 10 copies are made.

The AUTOEXEC.BAT File

The AUTOEXEC.BAT file is a batch file that is automatically executed whenever DOS is started. If a diskette contains a file with the name AUTOEXEC.BAT, then it is executed on DOS startup without any operator action. For example, suppose that you want your PC to start BASIC automatically whenever DOS is started. Just create a diskette file called AUTOEXEC.BAT containing the command

```
BASIC
```

Note that you may have only one AUTOEXEC.BAT file on a given diskette. On the other hand, you may have many batch files.

> **TEST YOUR UNDERSTANDING 2 (answer on page 57)**
>
> Modify your DOS diskette so that BASIC is started whenever you start DOS.

The AUTOEXEC.BAT file may be used for some clever purposes. For example, let's return to our company with 10 managers. Suppose that you wish to include a covering memo that reads

```
TO:MANAGERS
HERE ARE THE STATEMENTS FOR MAY.
WE'LL MEET TO DISCUSS THEM ON 6/4
AT 5:30 pm.
        JR
```

Here is how the message can be automatically displayed:

1. Create a file on your diskette which contains the text of the message. Call the file MSSG .
2. Create a file AUTOEXEC.BAT that contains the DOS command
    TYPE MSSG
3. Modify the batch file C.BAT so that it copies MSSG and AUTOEXEC.BAT onto each of the 10 copies.

Each manager will start his or her PC using a duplicate diskette. The AUTOEXEC.BAT file will cause the file MSSG to be displayed on the screen.

Parameters

Let's stick with our fictitious company. Suppose that the 10 diskettes are to be prepared and sent every month. The file names are always the same, but the month abbreviations, as given in the file name extensions, vary. You could prepare a new batch file C.BAT every month. However, there is a better way. Designate the month abbreviation by the symbol **%1**. (% is an abbreviation for **parameter** and 1 is the number of the parameter.) The commands of the batch file are then written:

```
FORMAT B:/S
COPY A:ACCOUNTS.%1 B:
COPY A:PROFIT.%1 B:
COPY A:PAYABLE.%1 B:
COPY A:SALES.%1 B:
```

For the month of MAY, we would give the batch command

```
C MAY
```

For the month of JUNE, give the batch command

```
C JUN
```

And so forth.

You may use up to nine parameters %1,%2, . . .,%9. You specify the values of these parameters when you give the batch command with consecutive parameter values separated by spaces. For example, if a batch

3.8 Creating Your Own DOS Commands—Batch Files

file D used the two parameters %1 and %2, then to execute the batch file with %1 = JAN and %2 = FEB, we would use the command

```
D JAN FEB
```

ANSWERS TO TEST YOUR UNDERSTANDINGS 1 and 2

1: Add the DOS commands

```
COMP A:ACCOUNTS.MAY B:
COMP A:PROFIT.MAY B:
COMP A:PAYABLE.MAY B:
COMP A:SALES.MAY B:
```

2: Add the file AUTOEXEC.BAT that consists of the single DOS command

```
BASIC
```

II

An Introduction to PC BASIC

Getting Started in BASIC

4

4.1 Beginning BASIC

In Chapter 2 we learned to manipulate the keyboard and display screen of the IBM Personal Computer. Let's now learn how to communicate instructions to the computer.

Just as humans use languages to communicate with one another, computers use languages to communicate with other electronic devices (such as printers), human operators, and even other computers. There are hundreds of computer languages in use today, and your IBM Personal Computer is capable of "speaking" quite a few of them. Among these languages BASIC is both versatile and very easy to learn. It was developed especially for computer novices by John Kemeny and Thomas Kurtz at Dartmouth College. In the next few chapters we will concentrate on learning the fundamentals of BASIC. In the process we will learn a great deal about the ways a computer may be used to solve problems.

The IBM Personal Computer actually comes with three different versions of the BASIC language. The least powerful version of BASIC is called **cassette BASIC**. This is the BASIC version that is supplied with all IBM Personal Computers and is stored in ROM. If you equip your computer with one or more diskette drives, you are able to make use of a more powerful language called **diskette BASIC**. This version includes all the commands of cassette BASIC plus additional commands that allow you to make use of your diskette drives. The third level of BASIC is called **BASICA** (short for **Advanced BASIC**) and includes all of the commands of diskette BASIC. In addition, Advanced BASIC provides commands to perform advanced graphics functions, play music, and control various optional devices, such as game paddles and a light pen. (Note, however, that many statements of Advanced BASIC require that the computer be equipped with the color/graphics interface.)

The instructions in Chapter 1 allow you to load diskette BASIC. For the next few chapters we will concentrate on the commands provided in this version of BASIC. Later on we will discuss some of the enhancements provided by Advanced BASIC. We will ignore cassette BASIC.

4.2 Running BASIC Programs

A sequence of computer instructions is called a **program**. We will learn to write programs that do arithmetic, draw charts, and even play tic tac toe. Before we go off to write our own programs, however, let's look at one that IBM has prepared to demonstrate the power of their computer.

Insert your DOS diskette (the copy, not the original) into drive A: , start the computer, and obtain the BASIC prompt Ok, as described in Chapter 1. IBM has included many interesting programs on the diskette. To obtain a list of these programs, type

```
FILES
```

4.2 Running BASIC Programs

and press ENTER. The names of the programs on the diskette will be displayed on the screen.

One of the most impressive programs is MUSIC. (Note that it is listed under the name MUSIC. BAS. The extension BAS indicates that the program is written in BASIC.) To load the program MUSIC from the diskette into RAM, type

```
LOAD "MUSIC"
```

and press ENTER. (Note the quotation marks.) The diskette drive light will go on, you will hear the drive at work, and the program MUSIC will be loaded into RAM. The drive light will then go out and the drive will stop.

Let's now make the computer perform the instructions in the program. (In computer jargon, we **run the program**.) Type

```
RUN
```

and press ENTER. The computer draws a piano keyboard on the screen and displays the names of some songs. To play a song, press the key indicated. Why not spend a few minutes enjoying the computer-generated music. Note also how the computer "animates" the keyboard by displaying a moving note, which indicates the key being played.

Sooner or later you will want to interrupt a computer program while it is running. This is done by **simultaneously** pressing the Ctrl and Break keys. It's a two-handed operation and with good reason. The keys are arranged so that you won't interrupt programs accidentally. To illustrate how you may interrupt a program, run MUSIC and play a song. In the middle of the song, simultaneously hit Ctrl and Break. The program will stop. The screen will display a message of this sort:

```
Break in line xxxx
Ok
■
```

The line xxxx gives the place in the program where you stopped the computer. (We'll learn about line numbers in the next section.) The BASIC prompt Ok indicates that BASIC is awaiting another command. Interrupting a program does not erase it from RAM. To run the program again, just type RUN and press ENTER.

Well, enough music for now! Let's end the program. According to the instructions on the screen, you may "EXIT" the program by pressing Esc, a key which is located on the upper left side of the keyboard. Press this key. Note that the BASIC prompt Ok is displayed, indicating that BASIC is awaiting a command.

You probably are curious to see the set of instructions which comprise MUSIC. Nothing could be easier. Type

```
LIST
```

and press ENTER. You will see the instructions of the program displayed on the screen. Of course, they are going by too quickly to read them.

Later we'll learn how to stop the display where we want or to obtain a written copy on the printer.

TEST YOUR UNDERSTANDING 1 (answer on page 64)

Pick out a program on the DOS diskette, load it into memory and run it. (Some programs may require the color/graphics adapter. Don't worry. If you don't have this circuit board installed, the computer will tell you that it can't run the program and will redisplay the BASIC prompt.)

ANSWER TO TEST YOUR UNDERSTANDING 1

1: Start from the BASIC prompt. Type LOAD <program name> and press ENTER. Here <program name> is the name of the program you wish to run. Omit the extension BAS. Now type RUN and press ENTER.

4.3 Writing BASIC Programs

You may be intimidated by the number of instructions in the program MUSIC. Don't be. In no time at all you will be writing programs just as complicated. But let's take one step at a time and first learn to write some simple BASIC programs.

Assume that you have followed the start-up instructions of Chapter 1 and the computer shows it is ready to accept further instructions by displaying the BASIC prompt

```
Ok
```

From this point on a typical session with your computer might go like this:

1. Type in a program.
2. Locate and correct any errors in the program.
3. Run the program.
4. Obtain the output requested by the program.
5. Either: (a) run the program again; or (b) repeat steps 1-4 for a new program; or (c) end the programming session (turn off the computer and go have lunch).

To fully understand what is involved in these five steps, let us consider a particular example. Suppose that you want the computer to add 5 and 7. First, you would type the following instructions:

```
10 PRINT 5 + 7
20 END
```

This sequence of two instructions constitutes a program to calculate 5 + 7. Note that as you type the program the computer records your instructions **but does not carry them out**. As you are typing a program, the computer provides you with an opportunity to change, delete, and correct instruction lines. (More on how to do this later.) Once you are content with your program, tell the computer to run it (that is, to execute the instructions) by typing the command*:

```
RUN
```

The computer will run the program and display the desired answer:

```
12
```

If you wish the computer to run the program a second time, type **RUN** again.

Running a program does not erase it from RAM. Therefore, if you wish to add instructions to the program or change the program, you may continue typing just as if the RUN command had not intervened. For example, if you wish to include in your program the problem of calculating 5 − 7, we type the additional line

```
15 PRINT 5 - 7
```

To see the program currently in memory, type **LIST** (no line number), then hit the ENTER key. The program consists of the following three lines, now displayed on the screen:

```
10 PRINT 5 + 7
15 PRINT 5 - 7
20 END
```

Note how the computer puts line 15 in proper sequence. If we now type RUN again, the computer will display the two answers:

```
12
-2
```

In the event that you now wish to go on to another program, type the command

```
NEW
```

This erases the previous program from RAM and prepares the computer to accept a new program. You should always remember the following important fact:

> **RAM can contain only one program at a time.**

---

*Don't forget to follow the command with **ENTER**. Recall that the computer will not recognize lines unless they have been sent to it by hitting the **ENTER** key.

Getting Started in BASIC

> **TEST YOUR UNDERSTANDING 1 (answers on page 67)**
>
> a. Write and type in a BASIC program to calculate 12.1 + 98 + 5.32.
> b. Run the program of a.
> c. Erase the program of a from RAM.
> d. Write a program to calculate 48.75 − 1.674.
> e. Type in and run the program of d.

Command Mode and Execute Mode

BASIC on the IBM Personal Computer operates in two distinct modes. In **command mode** the computer accepts typed program lines and commands (like **RUN** and **NEW**) used to manipulate programs. The computer identifies a program line by its line number. Program lines are not immediately executed. Rather, they are stored in RAM until you tell the computer what to do with them. On the other hand, commands are executed as soon as they are given.

In the **execute mode** the computer runs a program. In this mode the screen is under control of the program.

When you turn the computer on it is automatically in command mode, indicated by the presence of the **Ok** prompt on the screen. The RUN command puts the computer into execute mode. After the computer finishes running a program, it redisplays the **Ok** prompt indicating that it is back in command mode.

Upper Case vs Lower Case and Extra Spaces

The computer is a stern taskmaster! It has a very limited vocabulary (BASIC) and this vocabulary must be used according to very specific rules concerning the order of words, punctuation, and so forth. However, BASIC allows for some freedom of expression. For example, BASIC commands may be typed in capitals, lower case, or a mixture of the two. Also, any extra spaces are ignored. Thus, BASIC will interpret all of the following instructions as the same:

```
10 PRINT A
10 print a
10 Print A
10 print      A
10       print A
```

Note that BASIC expects spaces in certain places. For example, there must be a space separating PRINT and A in the above command. Otherwise, BASIC will read the command as PRINTA, which is not in its vocabulary!

A Word of Warning

Many people think of a computer as an "electronic brain" that somehow has the power of human thought. This is very far from the truth. The electronics of the computer and the rules of the BASIC language allow it to recognize a very limited vocabulary and to take various actions based on the data that is given to it. It is very important to realize that the computer does not have "common sense." The computer will attempt to interpret whatever data you input. If what you input is a recognizable command, the computer will perform it. It does not matter that the command makes no sense in a particular context. The computer has no way to make such judgments. It can only do what you instruct it to do. Because of the computer's inflexibility in interpreting commands, you must tell the computer **exactly** what you want it to do. Don't worry about confusing the computer. If you communicate a command in an incorrect form, you won't damage the machine in any way! However, in order to make the machine do our bidding, it is necessary to learn to speak its language precisely.

ANSWERS TO TEST YOUR UNDERSTANDING 1

1: a. `10 PRINT 12.1 + 98 + 5.32`
      `20 END`
   b. Type RUN and press ENTER.
   c. Type NEW and press ENTER.
   d. `10 PRINT 48.75 - 1.674`
      `20 END`
   e. Type in the program. Type RUN and press ENTER.

4.4 Some Elementary BASIC Programs

In learning to use a language, you must first learn the alphabet of the language. Next, you must learn the vocabulary of the language. Finally, you must study the way in which words are put together into sentences. In learning the BASIC language, we will follow the progression just described. In Chapter 2 we learned about the characters of the IBM Personal Computer keyboard. These characters are the alphabet of BASIC. Let us now learn some basic vocabulary. The simplest "words" are the so-called constants.

BASIC Constants

BASIC allows us to manipulate numbers and text. The rules for manipulating numerical data differ from those for handling text, however.

Getting Started in BASIC

In BASIC we distinguish between these two types of data as follows: a **numeric constant** is a number and a **string constant** is a sequence of keyboard characters, which may include letters, numbers, or any other keyboard symbols. The following are examples of numeric constants:

5, −2, 3.145, 23456, 456.78345676543987, 27134566543

The following are examples of string constants:

"John", "Accounts Receivable", "$234.45 Due", "Dec. 4,1981"

Note that string constants are always enclosed in quotation marks. In order to avoid vagueness, quotation marks may not appear as part of a string constant. (In practice, an apostrophe (') should be used as a substitute for a quotation mark (") within a string constant.) Numbers may appear within a string constant, such as "$45.30". However, you cannot use such numbers in arithmetic. Only numbers not enclosed by quotation marks may be used for arithmetic.

In many applications it is necessary to refer to a string constant that has no characters within its quotation marks, namely the string "". This string constant is called the **null string**.

For certain applications you may wish to specify your numeric constants in **exponential format**. This will be especially helpful in the case of very large and very small numbers. Consider the number 15,300,000,000. It is very inconvenient to type all the zeros. It can be written in the handy shorthand as 1.53E10. The 1.53 indicates the first three digits of the number. The E10 means that you move the decimal point in the 1.53 to the right 10 places. Similarly, the number −237,000 may be written in the exponential format as −2.37E5. The exponential format may also be used for very small numbers. For example, the number .00000000054 may be written in exponential format as 5.4E−10. The −10 indicates that the decimal point in 5.4 is to be moved 10 places to the *left*.

TEST YOUR UNDERSTANDING 1 (answers on page 75)

    a. Write these numbers in exponential format: .00048 and −1374.5
    b. Write these numbers in decimal format: −9.7E3, 9.7E−3, and −9.7E−3

BASIC Programs

Let us look again at the BASIC program in Section 4.3, namely:

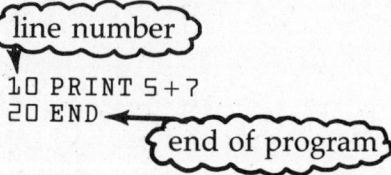

(line number)

```
10 PRINT 5+7
20 END
```

(end of program)

4.4 Some Elementary BASIC Programs

This program illustrates two very important features common to all BASIC programs:

1. The instructions of a program must be numbered. Each line must start with a line number. The computer executes instructions in order of increasing line number.
2. The **END** instruction identifies the end of the program. On encountering this instruction, the computer stops running the program and displays Ok, indicating that BASIC has returned to the command mode.

Note that line numbers need not be consecutive. For example, it is perfectly acceptable to have a program whose line numbers are 10, 23, 47, 55, or 100. Also note that it is not necessary to type instructions in their numerical order. You could type line 20 and then go back and type line 10. The computer will sort out the lines and rearrange them according to increasing number. This feature is especially helpful in case you accidentally omit a line while typing your program.

Here is another important fact about line numbering. If you type two lines having the same line number, the computer erases the first version and remembers the second version. This feature is very useful for correcting errors: If a line has an error, just retype it and press ENTER.

Your IBM Personal Computer will perform all the standard calculations that can be done with a calculator. Since most people are familiar with the operation of a calculator, let us start by writing programs to solve various arithmetic problems.

Most arithmetic operations are written in customary fashion. For example, addition and subtraction are written for the computer in the usual way:

$5 + 4, 9 - 8$

Multiplication, however, is typed using the symbol * , which shares the "8" key. As an example, the product of 5 and 3 is typed

5*3

Division is typed using a slash (/). For example, 8.2 divided by 15 is typed

8.2/15

Example 1. Write a BASIC program to calculate the sum of 54.75, 78.83, and 548.

Solution. The sum is indicated by typing

54.75 + 78.83 + 548

The BASIC instruction for printing data on the screen is **PRINT**, so we write our program as follows:

```
10 PRINT 54.75 + 78.83 + 548
20 END
```

70   Getting Started in BASIC

BASIC carries out arithmetic operations in a special order. It scans an expression and carries out all multiplication and division operations first, *proceeding in left-to-right order*. It then returns to the left side of the expression and performs addition and subtraction, also in a left-to-right order. If parentheses occur, these are evaluated first, following the same rules stated above. If parentheses occur within parentheses, the innermost parentheses are evaluated first.

Example 2. What numerical values will BASIC calculate from these expressions?

    a. (5 + 7)/2   b. 5 + 7/2
    c. 5 + 7*3/2   d. (5 + 7*3)/2

Solution.

  a. The computer first applies its rules for the order of calculation to determine the value in the parentheses, namely 12. It then divides 12 by 2 to obtain 6.
  b. The computer scans the expression from left to right performing all multiplication and division in the order encountered. First it divides 7 by 2 to obtain 3.5. It then rescans the line and performs all additions and subtractions in order. This gives us

```
5 + 3.5 = 8.5
```

  c. The computer first performs all multiplication and division in order:

```
5 + 10.5
```

    Now it performs addition to obtain 15.5.
  d. The computer calculates the value of all parentheses first. In this case, it computes 5 + 7*3 = 26. (Note that it does the multiplication first!) Next it rescans the line which now looks like this:

```
26/2
```

It performs the division to obtain 13.

TEST YOUR UNDERSTANDING 2 (answer on page 75)

Calculate 5+3/2+2 and (5+3)/(2+2).

Example 3. Write a BASIC program to calculate the quantity

$$\frac{22 \times 18 + 34 \times 11 - 12.5 \times 8}{27.8}$$

Solution. Here is the program:

```
10 PRINT (22*18 + 34*11 - 12.5*8)/27.8
20 END
```

4.4 Some Elementary BASIC Programs

Note that we used parentheses in line 10. They tell the computer that the entire quantity in parentheses is to be divided by 27.8. If we had omitted the parentheses, the computer would divide $-12.5*8$ by 27.8 and add $22*18$ and $34*11$ to the result.

TEST YOUR UNDERSTANDING 3 (answers on page 75)

Write BASIC programs to calculate:
  a. $((4\times 3 + 5\times 8 + 7\times 9)/(7\times 9 + 4\times 3 + 8\times 7)) \times 48.7$
  b. 27.8 % of $(112 + 38 + 42)$
  c. The average of the numbers 88, 78, 84, 49, 63

Printing Words

So far we have used the **PRINT** statement only to display the answers to numerical problems. However, this instruction is very versatile. It also allows us to display string constants. For example, consider this instruction:

```
10 PRINT "Patient History"
```

During program execution, this statement will create the following display:

```
Patient History
```

In order to display several string constants on the same line, separate them by commas in a single **PRINT** statement. For example, consider the instruction

```
10 PRINT "AGE", "SEX", "BIRTHPLACE","ADDRESS"
```

It will cause four words to be printed as follows:

```
AGE    SEX     BIRTHPLACE    ADDRESS
```

Both numeric constants and string constants may be included in a single **PRINT** statement. For example,

```
100 PRINT "AGE", 65.43, "NO. DEPENDENTS"
```

Here is how the computer determines the spacing on a line as follows. Each line is divided into print zones. The first five print zones each have 14 spaces and the sixth 10 spaces. By placing a comma in a PRINT statement, you are telling the computer to start the next string of text at the beginning of the next print zone. Thus, for example, the four words above begin in columns 1, 15, 29, 44 respectively. (See Figure 4-1.)

72   Getting Started in BASIC

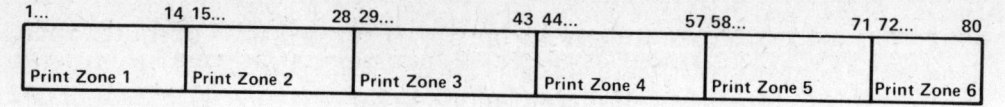

```
1...        14 15...      28 29...      43 44...      57 58...      71 72...     80
┌─────────────┬─────────────┬─────────────┬─────────────┬─────────────┬─────────────┐
│ Print Zone 1│ Print Zone 2│ Print Zone 3│ Print Zone 4│ Print Zone 5│ Print Zone 6│
└─────────────┴─────────────┴─────────────┴─────────────┴─────────────┴─────────────┘
```

Figure 4-1. Print zones.

TEST YOUR UNDERSTANDING 4 (answer on page 75)

Write a program to print the following display.

```
                NAME
LAST        FIRST       MIDDLE      GRADE
SMITH       JOHN        DAVID       87
```

Example 4. Suppose that a distributor of office supplies sells 50 chairs and 5 desks. The chairs cost $59.70 each and are subject to a 30% discount. The desks cost $247.90 each and are also subject to a 30% discount. Prepare a bill for the shipment.

Solution. Let us insert four headings on our bill: Item, Quantity, Price, and Cost. We then print two lines corresponding to the two types of items shipped. Finally, we calculate the total due as shown here.

```
10 PRINT "ITEM","QTY","PRICE","COST"
20 PRINT
30 PRINT "CHAIR",50,59.70,50*(59.70-.3*59.70)
40 PRINT "DESK",5,247.90, 5*(247.90-.3*247.90)
50 PRINT
60 PRINT "TOTAL DUE",,,50*(59.70-.3*59.70)+5*
   (247.90-.3*247.90)
```

Note the **PRINT** statements in lines 20 and 50. They specify that a blank line is to be printed. Also note the series of three commas in line 60. The additional two commas move the next printing over to the beginning of the fourth print zone, which would bring the total cost directly under the column labeled "COST". If we now type **RUN** (followed by **ENTER**), the screen will look like this:

```
RUN
ITEM        QTY         PRICE       COST
CHAIR       50          59.70       2089.50
DESK        5           247.90      867.65
TOTAL DUE                           2957.15
```

You may think that the above invoice is somewhat sloppy because the columns of figures are not properly aligned. Patience! We will learn to align the columns after we have learned a bit more programming.

TEST YOUR UNDERSTANDING 5 (answer on page 75)

Write a computer program that creates the following display.

```
                         BUDGET-APRIL
    FOOD                 387.50
    CAR                  475.00
    GAS                  123.71
    UTILITIES            146.00
    ENTERTAINMENT        100.00
                         _____
    TOTAL                (Calculate total)
```

Exponentiation

Suppose that A is a number and N is a positive whole number (this means that N is one of the numbers 1,2,3,4,...). Then A **raised to the Nth power** is the product of A times itself N times. This quantity is usually denoted A^N, and the process of calculating it is called *exponentiation*. For example,

2^3 = 2*2*2 = 8, 5^7 = 5*5*5*5*5*5*5 = 78125.

It is possible to calculate A^N by repeated multiplication. However, if N is large, this can be tiresome to type. BASIC provides a shortcut for typing this function. Exponentiation is denoted by the symbol ^, which is produced by hitting the key with the upward-pointing arrow (this symbol shares the "6" key at the top of the keyboard). For example, 2^3 is denoted 2^3. The operation of exponentiation is done before multiplication and division. This is illustrated in the following example.

Example 5. Determine the value that BASIC assigns to this expression:

20*3 - 5*2^3

Solution. The exponentiation is performed first to yield:

20*3 - 5*8 = 60 - 40
           = 20

TEST YOUR UNDERSTANDING 6 (answers on page 75)

Evaluate the following first manually and then by an IBM Personal Computer program.

a. $2^4 \times 3$ b. $2^2 \times 3^3 - 12^2/3^2 \times 2$

74 Getting Started in BASIC

Exercises (answers on page 366)

Write BASIC programs to calculate the following quantities:
1. 57 + 23 + 48
2. 57.83 × (48.27 − 12.54)
3. 127.86/38
4. 365/.005 + 1.02^5
5. Make a table of the first, second, third, and fourth powers of the numbers 2, 3, 4, 5, and 6. Put all first powers in a column, all second powers in another column, and so forth.
6. Mrs. Anita Smith went to her doctor with a broken leg. Her bill consists of $45 for removal of the cast, $35 for therapy, and $5 for drugs. Her major medical policy will pay 80 percent directly to the doctor. Use the computer to prepare an invoice for Mrs. Smith.
7. A school board election is held to elect a representative for a district consisting of Wards 1,2,3, and 4. There are three candidates: Mr. Thacker, Ms. Hoving, and Mrs. Weatherby. The tallies by candidate and ward are as follows:

	Ward 1	Ward 2	Ward 3	Ward 4
Thacker	698	732	129	487
Hoving	148	928	246	201
Weatherby	379	1087	148	641

Write a BASIC computer program to calculate the total number of votes achieved by each candidate, as well as the total number of votes cast.

Describe the output from each of these programs.

8. ```
   10 PRINT 8*2 - 3*(2^4 - 10)
   20 END
   ```
9. ```
   10 PRINT "SILVER","GOLD","COPPER","PLATINUM"
   20 PRINT 327,448,1052,2
   30 END
   ```
10. ```
    10 PRINT , "GROCERIES","MEATS","DRUGS"
    20 PRINT "MON", "1,245","2,348","2,531"
    30 PRINT "TUE", "  248","3,459","2,148"
    40 END
    ```

Convert the following numbers to exponential format:

11. 23,000,000
12. 175.25
13. −200,000,000
14. .00014
15. −.000000000275
16. 53,420,000,000,000,000
    ```

Convert the following numbers in exponential format to standard format.

17. 1.59E5
18. −20.3456E6
19. −7.456E−12
20. 2.39456E−18

ANSWERS TO TEST YOUR UNDERSTANDINGS 1, 2, 3, 4, 5, and 6

1: a. 4.8E−4, −1.3745E3
   b. −9700, .0097, −.0097
2: 8.5 and 2
3: a. ``10 PRINT ((4*3+5*8+7*9)/(7*9+4*3+8*7))*48.7``
      ``20 END``
   b. ``10 PRINT .278*(112+38+42)``
      ``20 END``
   c. ``10 PRINT (88+78+84+49+63)/5``
      ``20 END``
4: ``10 PRINT ,"NAME"``
   ``20 PRINT``
   ``30 PRINT "LAST","FIRST","MIDDLE","GRADE"``
   ``40 PRINT``
   ``50 PRINT "SMITH","JOHN","DAVID",87``
   ``60 END``
5: ``10 PRINT ,"    BUDGET-APRIL"``
   ``20 PRINT "FOOD", 387.50``
   ``30 PRINT "CAR",  475.00``
   ``40 PRINT "GAS",  123.71``
   ``50 PRINT "UTILITIES", 146.00``
   ``60 PRINT "ENTERTAINMENT", 100.00``
   ``70 PRINT , "_____"``
   ``80 PRINT "TOTAL", 387.50+475.00+123.71+146.00+``
   ``   100.00``
   ``90 END``
6: a. **48**
   b. **76**

4.5 Giving Names to Numbers and Words

In the examples and exercises of the preceding section, you probably noticed that you were wasting considerable time retyping certain numbers over and over. Not only does this retyping waste time, it is also a likely source for errors. Fortunately, such retyping is unnecessary if we use variables.

A **variable** is a letter that is used to represent a number. Any letter of the alphabet may be used as a variable. (There are other possible names for variables. See below.) Possible variables are A, B, C, X, Y, or Z. At any given moment, a variable has a particular value. For example, the variable A might have the value 5 while B might have the value −2.137845. One method for changing the value of a variable is through use of the **LET** statement. The statement

```
10 LET A=7
```

sets the value of A equal to 7. Any previous value of A is erased.

Once the value of a variable has been set, the variable may be used throughout the program. The computer will insert the appropriate value wherever the variable occurs. For instance, if A has the value 7 then the expression

```
A + 5
```

is evaluated as 7 + 5 or 12. The expression

```
3*A - 10
```

is evaluated 3*7 − 10 = 21 − 10 = 11. The expression 2*A^2 is evaluated

```
2*7^2 = 2*49 = 98
```

> **TEST YOUR UNDERSTANDING 1 (answer on page 84)**
>
> Suppose that A has the value 4 and B has the value 3. What is the value of the expression A^2/2*B^2 ?

Note the following important fact:

> **If you do not specify a value for a variable, BASIC will assign it the value Zero.**

Here are three useful shortcuts.

> **THREE SHORTCUTS**
>
> 1. The word LET is optional. For example, the statement
>
>    ```
>    10 LET A=5
>    ```
>
>   may be abbreviated as
>
>    ```
>    10 A=5
>    ```
>
> 2. Several statements may be included on one line. To do so, just separate the various statements by colons. In particular, a single line may be used to assign values to several variables. For instance, the instruction
>
>    ```
>    100 LET C=18: LET D=23: LET E=2.718
>    ```

assigns C the value 18, D the value 23, and E the value 2.718. Using shortcut 1, we may write this instruction in the simpler form:

```
100 C=18:D=23:E=2.718
```

3. You may use statements that extend beyond a single line. This is especially useful when assigning values to many variables as in shortcut 2 above. When you reach the end of the physical line (40 or 80 characters wide) just keep on typing. Hit ENTER when you are finished with the material to be included in the current line number. An extended line may contain as many as 255 characters. When an extended line reaches 255 characters, BASIC will automatically terminate it just as if you had pressed ENTER.

Variables in PRINT Statements

Variables may also be used in **PRINT** statements. For example, the statement

```
10 PRINT A
```

will cause the computer to print the current value of A (in the first print zone, of course!). The statement

```
20 PRINT A,B,C
```

will result in printing the current values of A, B, and C in print zones 1, 2 and 3, respectively.

> **TEST YOUR UNDERSTANDING 2 (answer on page 84)**
>
> Suppose that A has the value 5. What will be the result of the instruction
>
> ```
> 10 PRINT A,A^2,2*A^2
> ```

Example 1. Consider the three numbers 5.71, 3.23, and 4.05. Calculate their sum, their product, and the sum of their squares (i.e., the sum of their second powers; such a sum is often used in statistics.).

Solution. Introduce the variables A, B, and C and set them equal, respectively, to the three numbers. Then compute the desired quantities.

```
10 LET A=5.71: B=3.23: C=4.05
20 PRINT "THE SUM IS", A+B+C
30 PRINT "THE PRODUCT IS", A*B*C
40 PRINT "THE SUM OF SQUARES IS", A^2+B^2+C^2
50 END
```

78   Getting Started in BASIC

> **TEST YOUR UNDERSTANDING 3 (answer on page 84)**
>
> Consider the numbers 101, 102, 103, 104, 105, and 106. Write a program that calculates the product of the first two, the first three, the first four, the first five, and then all six numbers.

The following mental imagery is often helpful in understanding how BASIC handles variables. When BASIC first encounters a variable, let's say A, it sets up a box (actually a memory location) that it labels "A". (See Figure 4-2.) In this box it stores the current value of A. When you request a change in the value of A, the computer throws out the current contents of the box and inserts the new value.

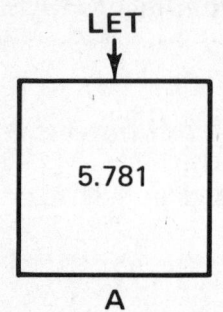

LET
↓

```
┌─────────┐
│         │
│  5.781  │
│         │
└─────────┘
     A
```

Figure 4-2. The variable A.

Note that the value of a variable need not remain the same throughout a program. At any point in the program you may change the value of a variable (with a **LET** statement, for example). If a program is called on to evaluate an expression involving a variable, it will always use the **current** value of the variable, ignoring any previous values the variable may have had at earlier points in the program.

> **TEST YOUR UNDERSTANDING 4 (answer on page 84)**
>
> Suppose that a loan for $5,000 has an interest rate of 1.5 percent on the unpaid balance at the end of each month. Write a program to calculate the interest at the end of the first month. Suppose that at the end of the first month you make a payment of $150 (after the interest is added). Design your program to calculate the balance after the payment. (Begin by letting B = the loan balance, IN = the interest, and P = the payment. After the payment the new balance is B+IN−P.)

Example 2. What will be the output of the following computer program?

```
10 LET A=10: B=20
20 LET A=5
30 PRINT A + B + C, A*B*C
40 END
```

Solution. Note that no value for C is specified, so C = 0. Also note that the value of A is initially set to 10. However, in line 20 this value is changed to 5. So in line 30 A, B and C have the respective values 5, 20, and 0. Therefore, the output will be

25   0

To the computer, the statement

LET A =

means that the current value of A is to be **replaced** with whatever appears to the right of the equal sign. Therefore, if we write

LET A = A + 1

we are asking the computer to replace the current value of A with A + 1. So if the current value of A is 4, the value of A after performing the instruction is 4 + 1, or 5.

> **TEST YOUR UNDERSTANDING 5 (answer on page 84)**
> What is the output of the following program?
> ```
> 10 LET A = 5.3
> 20 LET A = A + 1
> 30 LET A = 2 * A
> 40 LET A = A + B
> 50 PRINT A
> 60 END
> ```

Legal Variable Names

As we mentioned previously, you may use any letter of the alphabet as a variable name. The IBM Personal Computer is quite flexible concerning variable names. A variable name must begin with a letter and may contain as many as 40 characters. Therefore, you may use variables named PAYROLL, TAX, REFUND, and BALANCE. Actually, not every sequence of characters is a legal variable name. You must avoid any sequences of characters that are reserved by BASIC for special meanings. Examples of such words are:

IF, ON, OR, TO, THEN, GOTO

Once you become familiar with BASIC, it will be second nature to avoid these and the other reserved words as variable names.

A variable name *cannot* begin with a number. For example, 1A is *not* a legal variable name. If you attempt to use a variable name that begins with a number, BASIC will provide an error message.

String Variables

So far, all of the variables we have discussed have represented numerical values. However, BASIC also allows variables to assume string constants (sequences of characters) as values. The variables for doing this are called *string variables* and are denoted by a variable name followed by a dollar sign ($). Thus, **A$**, **B1$**, and **ZZ$** are all valid names of string variables. To assign a value to a string variable we use the **LET** statement with the desired value inserted in quotation marks after the equal sign. To set A$ equal to the string "Balance Sheet", we use the statement

```
LET A$="Balance Sheet"
```

We may print the value of a string variable just as we print the value of a numeric variable. For example, if A$ has the value just assigned, the statement

```
PRINT A$
```

will result in the following screen output:

```
Balance Sheet
```

Example 3. What will be the output of the following program?

```
10 LET A$="MONTHLY RECEIPTS":B$="MONTHLY
   EXPENSES"
20 LET A=20373.10: B=17584.31
30 PRINT A$,B$
40 PRINT A,,B
50 END
```

Solution. Line 30 prints the values of the two string variables A$ and B$, namely "MONTHLY RECEIPTS" and "MONTHLY EXPENSES" at the beginning of two print zones. Since "MONTHLY RECEIPTS" is more than 14 characters (print zones are 14 characters wide), the string "MONTHLY EXPENSES" is placed at the beginning of print zone three. Line 40 displays the values of A and B. We have inserted an extra comma in line 40 to push the value of B over to the beginning of print zone three. Moreover, since the values of A and B are positive numbers, they begin with a blank space. Here is the output of the program:

```
MONTHLY RECEIPTS     MONTHLY EXPENSES
  20373.10             17584.31
```

Note that we have used the variables A and A$ (as well as B and B$) in the same program. The variables A and A$ are considered *different* by the computer. Also note the presence of the second comma in line 40. This is due to the fact that the value of A$, MONTHLY RECEIPTS, requires 16 spaces. Therefore, to leave a space between the two headings, we moved B$ over into the next print zone. To correctly align the values of A and B under the appropriate headings, we must print a blank space in print zone two after we print the value of A. This is accomplished by the second comma. One further comment about spacing. Note that the numbers do not exactly align with the headings but are offset by one space. This is because BASIC allows room for a sign (+ or −) in front of a number. In the case of positive numbers, the sign is left out but the space remains.

The SWAP Statement

Suppose that your program involves the two variables A and B and that you wish to reassign the values of these variables so that A assumes the value of B and B the value of A. This may be accomplished using the BASIC statement

```
10 SWAP A, B
```

For example, if A currently has the value 1.8 and B the value 7.5, then after the above statement is executed, A will have the value 7.5 and B the value 1.8.

Note that SWAP may also be used to exchange the values of two string variables, as in the statement

```
20 SWAP A$, B$
```

However, you may never SWAP values between a string variable and a numeric variable. BASIC will report an error if you try this.

TEST YOUR UNDERSTANDING 6 (answer on page 84)

Write a BASIC program to exchange the values of the variables A and B without using the SWAP statement. (It's tricky. That's why BASIC includes the SWAP statement.)

Remarks in Programs

It is very convenient to explain programs using remarks. For one thing, remarks make programs easier to read for a human being. Remarks also assist in finding errors and making modifications in a program. To insert a remark in a program we may use the **REM** statement. For example, consider the line

```
520 REM X DENOTES THE STAR SHIP POSITION
```

Since the line starts with **REM**, it will be ignored during program execution. As a substitute for REM, we may use an apostrophe as in the following example:

```
1040 ' Y IS THE LASER FORCE
```

To insert a remark on the same line as a program statement, use a colon followed by an apostrophe (or **REM**) as in this example:

```
10 LET A=PI*R^2 : ' A IS THE AREA,R IS THE RADIUS
```

Note, that everything after an apostrophe is ignored. Therefore, you cannot put an instruction after a remark. In the line

```
20 LET B=A^2: 'B is the area: C=B+8
```

the instruction C=B+8 will be ignored.

The importance of remarks cannot be overemphasized. In writing BASIC programs, it is all too easy to write programs that no one (you included) can decipher. You should aim at writing programs that can be read like text. The most significant step in this direction is to include many remarks in your programs. In what follows, we will be generous in our use of remarks, not only to make our programs easier to read, but also to set an example of good programming style.

> **TEST YOUR UNDERSTANDING 7 (answer on page 84)**
>
> What is the result of the following program line?
>
> ```
> 10 LET A=7:B$="COST":C$="TOTAL":PRINT C$,B$,"=",A
> ```

Using a Printer

In writing programs and analyzing their output, it is often easier to rely on written output rather than output on the screen. In computer terminology written output is called **hard copy** that may be provided by a wide variety of printers, ranging from a dot-matrix printer costing only a few hundred dollars to a daisy wheel printer costing several thousand dollars. As you begin to make serious use of your computer, you will find it difficult to do without hard copy. Indeed, writing programs is much easier if you can consult a hard copy listing of your program at various stages of program development. (One reason is that in printed output you are not confined to looking at your program in 25 line "snapshots.") Also, you will want to use the printer to produce output of programs ranging from tables of numerical data to address lists and text files.

You may produce hard copy on your printer by using the BASIC statement **LPRINT**. For example, the statement

```
10 LPRINT A,A$
```

will print the current values of A and A$ on the printer in print zones one and two. (As is the case with the screen, BASIC divides the printer line into print zones which are 14 columns wide.) Moreover, the statement

```
20 LPRINT "Customer","Credit Limit","Most Recent Pchs"
```

4.5 Giving Names to Numbers and Words

will result in printing three headings in the first three print zones, namely:

```
Customer       Credit Limit      Most Recent Pchs
```

Printing on the printer proceeds very much like printing on the screen. It is important to realize, however, that in order to print on both the screen *and* the printer, it is necessary to use *both* statements **PRINT** and **LPRINT**. For example, to print the values of A and A$ on both the screen and the printer, we must give two instructions as follows:

```
10 PRINT A,A$
20 LPRINT A,A$
```

Exercises (answers on page 367)

In Exercises 1-6, determine the output of the given program.

1. ```
   10 LET A=5:B=5
   20 PRINT A + B
   30 END
   ```
2. ```
   10 LET AA=5
   20 PRINT AA*B
   30 END
   ```
3. ```
   10 LET A1=5
   20 PRINT A1^2 +5*A1
   30 END
   ```
4. ```
   10 LET A=2: B=7: C=9
   20 PRINT A+B, A-C, A*C
   30 END
   ```
5. ```
   10 LET A$="JOHN JONES"
   20 LET B$="AGE": C=38
   30 PRINT A$, B$, C
   40 END
   ```
6. ```
   10 LET X=11: Y=19
   20 PRINT 2*X
   30 PRINT 3*Y
   40 END
   ```

What is wrong with the following BASIC statements?

7. `10 LET A="YOUTH"`
8. `10 LET AA=-12`
9. `10 LET A$=57`
10. `LET ZZ$=Address`
11. `250 LET AAA=-9`
12. `10000 LET 1A=-2.34567`

13. Consider the numbers 2.3758, 4.58321, and 58.11. Write a program that computes their sum, product, and the sum of their squares.
14. A company has three divisions: Office Supplies, Computers, and Newsletters. The revenues of these three divisions for the preceding quarter were, respectively, $346,712, $459,321, and $376,872. The expenses for the quarter were $176,894, $584,837, and $402,195, respectively. Write a program that displays this data on the screen, with appropriate explanatory headings. Your program should also compute and display the net profit (loss) from each division and the net profit (loss) for the company as a whole.

ANSWERS TO TEST YOUR UNDERSTANDING 1, 2, 3, 4, 5, 6, and 7

1: 72
2: It prints the display:
    5   25   50
3: 10 LET A=101:B=102:C=103:D=104:E=105:F=106
   20 PRINT A*B
   30 PRINT A*B*C
   40 PRINT A*B*C*D
   50 PRINT A*B*C*D*E
   60 PRINT A*B*C*D*E*F
   70 END
4: 10 LET B=5000: I=.015: P=150.00
   20 IN=I*B
   30 PRINT "INTEREST EQUALS", IN
   40 B=B+IN
   50 PRINT " BALANCE WITH INTEREST EQUALS", B
   60 B=B − P
   70 PRINT "BALANCE AFTER PAYMENT EQUALS", B
   80 END
5: 12.6
6: 10 TEMPORARY=A
   20 A=B
   30 B=TEMPORARY
7: It creates the display:
        TOTAL   COST   =   7

4.6 Some BASIC Commands

Thus far, most of our attention has been focused on learning statements to insert **inside** programs. Let us now learn a few of the commands available for **manipulating** programs and the computer. The **NEW** command, previously discussed, is in this category. Remember the following facts about BASIC commands.

BASIC Commands

1. Commands are typed *without* using a line number.
2. You must press the **ENTER** key after typing a command.
3. A command may be given whenever the computer is in the command mode. (Recall that whenever the computer enters the command mode, it displays the **Ok** message. The computer remains in the command mode until a **RUN** command is given.)
4. The computer executes commands as soon as they are received.

Listing a Program

To obtain a list of all program lines of the current program in RAM, you may type the command

```
LIST <ENTER>
```

For example, suppose that RAM contains the following program.

```
10 PRINT 5+7, 5-7
20 PRINT 5*7,5/7
30 END
```

(This program may or may not be currently displayed on the screen.) If you type **LIST**, then the above three instruction lines will be displayed, followed by the **Ok** message.

In developing a program, you will often find that it is necessary to add program lines to sections of the program already written. This will require you to input lines in non-consecutive order. Also, it may be necessary to correct lines already input. In either event, the screen will often not indicate the current version of the program. Typing **LIST** every so often will assist in keeping track of what has been changed. LISTing is particularly helpful in checking a program or determining why a program won't run.

Note that the IBM Personal Computer screen can display up to 25 lines of text. This means you can display only 25 program statements at one time. To **LIST** only those statements with line numbers from 1 to 25, we use the command

```
LIST 1-25 <ENTER>
```

In a similar fashion, we may list any collection of consecutive program lines.

There are several other variations of the **LIST** command. To list the program lines from the beginning of the program to line 75, use the command

```
LIST -75 <ENTER>
```

Similarly, to list the program lines from 100 to the end of the program, use the command

```
LIST 100- <ENTER>
```

To list line 100 use the command

```
LIST 100 <ENTER>
```

TEST YOUR UNDERSTANDING 1 (answers on page 90)

Write a command to:
a. List line 200 b. List lines 300-330 c. List lines 300 to the end
Test out these commands with a program.

HELPFUL SHORTCUT

If you press function key F1 and then ENTER, the PC will display a listing of the current program.

Printed Listings

You will find that it is difficult to write a long program relying only on screen listings. For more complex programs, a printed listing is essential. You may generate such a listing using your printer. To list the program currently in RAM, type

```
LLIST
```

and press ENTER. All the variations of the LIST command also apply to the LLIST command. For example, you may list only those lines with line numbers in a certain range, lines from the beginning of the program to a given line number, and so forth.

Deleting Program Lines

When typing a program or revising an existing program, it is often necessary to delete lines that are already part of the program. One simple way is to type the line number followed by **ENTER**. For example,

```
275
```

(followed by hitting the **ENTER** key) will delete line 275. The **DELETE** command may also by used for the same purpose. For example, we may delete line 275 using the command

```
DELETE 275 <ENTER>
```

The **DELETE** command has a number of variations that make it quite flexible. For example, to delete lines 200 to 500 inclusive, use the command

```
DELETE 200-500 <ENTER>
```

To delete all lines from the beginning of the program to 350, inclusive, use the command

```
DELETE -350 <ENTER>
```

Note that the **DELETE** command must always include a last line number to be deleted. This is to prevent unfortunate mishaps where you mistakenly erase most of a program. If you wish to delete all lines from 100 to the end of the program, you must specify a deletion from 100 to the last line number. If you don't remember the last line number, **LIST** the program first, determine the final line number, then carry out the appropriate **DELETE**.

4.6 Some BASIC Commands 87

HELPFUL SHORTCUT

If your program is long, you may want to avoid listing it in order to determine the number of the last line. Here is how to delete to the end of the program without listing it. The largest possible line number is 65535. Therefore, type

```
65535 END
```

and give the command

```
DELETE 100-65535
```

TEST YOUR UNDERSTANDING 2 (answers on page 90)

What is wrong with the following commands?

    a. DELETE 450-   b. LIST 450-   c. DELETE 300-200

Saving a Program

Once you have typed a program into RAM, you may save a copy on diskette. At any future time you may read the diskette copy back into RAM. At that point you may re-execute the program, modify it, or add to it. For the sake of concreteness, suppose that the following program is in RAM:

```
10 PRINT 5+7
20 END
```

Program Names. In order to save a program, we must first assign the program a name. A program name is a string of letters or numbers and may contain as many as eight characters. In addition, you may include an extension consisting of a period followed by three characters. If you specify more than eight characters in a program name, character 9, 10 and 11 are assumed to be an extension. Here are some valid program names:

    ACCOUNTING1 , GAMES.JOE , STORY.003

The first program name is equivalent to

    ACCOUNTI.NG1

If you do not specify an extension in a program name, then BASIC will automatically add the extension .BAS.

Saving Programs. Suppose that we choose the name RETAIN for our program. We may save this program on the diskette in either disk drive. To save RETAIN on drive B:, for example, we would use the command

    SAVE "B:RETAIN"

When the computer finishes writing a copy of the program onto the designated diskette, it will display the **Ok** prompt. Saving a program does not alter the copy of the program in RAM.

HELPFUL SHORTCUT

To save a program: press function key F4. BASIC will display

```
SAVE "
```

You may then fill in the program name and press ENTER.

Recalling a Program

To read a program from diskette into RAM, we use the LOAD command. For example, to read RETAIN from the diskette in drive B, we use the command:

```
LOAD "B:RETAIN"
```

You should try the above sequence of commands using the given program. After saving the program erase the program from RAM (by typing **NEW**). Then load the program. Just to check that the program has indeed been retrieved, you should now **LIST** it.

HELPFUL SHORTCUT

To load a program: Press function key F3. BASIC will display

```
LOAD "
```

You may then fill in the program name and press ENTER.

Erasing a Program From Diskette

You may erase a program from diskette by using the **KILL** command. To use this command you must recognize that if you specify no extension in your program name, BASIC will automatically add the extension .BAS. For example, the program RETAIN is actually stored under the name RETAIN.BAS . To erase this program you may use the command

```
KILL "B:RETAIN.BAS"
```

Manipulating Line Numbers

BASIC provides several commands that can ease your burden in dealing with line numbers.

4.6 Some BASIC Commands

The **AUTO** command may be used to automatically generate line numbers. To use this feature, type

```
AUTO
```

and press ENTER. BASIC will generate line numbers 10,20,30,40,... A line number will be displayed and the cursor moved to the second space after the line number. In response, type the corresponding program line. As usual, end the line by pressing ENTER. The computer will then automatically display the next line number.

To disable the AUTO feature simultaneously press the Ctrl and Break keys. The BASIC prompt will then be displayed.

You may have noticed that we always use line numbers that are multiples of 10. There is a good reason for this seeming "waste of line numbers." It is often necessary to add instructions between program lines. Our numbering scheme leaves rooms for up to nine such additions. (In between lines 40 and 50, for instance, we could add instruction lines 41, 42, . . ., 49.)

There are several useful variations of the AUTO command. You may start the automatic line number generation from any point. For example, to generate the line numbers

```
55,65,75,85, . . .,
```

use the command

```
AUTO 55
```

You may also adjust the spacing between line numbers. For example, to generate the sequence of line numbers

```
38,43,48,53,58, . . .,
```

which begins with 38 and has a spacing sequence of five, just use the command

```
AUTO 38,5
```

BASIC also has a provision for the automatic renumbering of lines. This is helpful, for example, when it is necessary to MERGE two programs whose line numbers overlap. The command

```
RENUM
```

causes BASIC to renumber all line numbers; the renumbered program will start with line 10 and use a spacing of 10. As with AUTO, the RENUM command has several useful variations. To renumber a program so that the line numbers begin with 1000, use the command

```
RENUM 1000
```

Renumbering may be restricted to a portion of the current program. To renumber lines 200 onward with the new line numbers beginning with 1000, use the command

```
RENUM 1000,200
```

All lines with numbers below 200 are not renumbered. You may even vary the spacing of the renumbered lines. To renumber lines 200 onward with the new line numbers beginning with 1000 having a spacing sequence of 100, use the command

```
RENUM 1000,200,100
```

To summarize, the general form of the RENUM command is

```
RENUM <new line>, <old line>, <increment>
```

Exercises (answers on page 367)

Exercises 1-9 refer to the following program.

```
10 LET A=19.1: B=17.5
20 PRINT A+B,A*B
30 END
```

1. Type the above program into RAM and RUN it. Use the AUTO feature to generate the line numbers.
2. Erase the screen without erasing RAM. LIST the program.
3. Save the program and erase RAM.
4. Recall the program and LIST it. RUN the program again.
5. Add the following line to the program:

```
25 PRINT A^2 + B^2
```

(Do not retype the entire program!) LIST and RUN the new program.
6. Save the new program without destroying the old one.
7. Recall the new program. Delete line 20 and RUN the resulting program.
8. Renumber the lines so that the lines numbers are 100,200,300.
9. Renumber the lines so that the line numbers are 10, 2000,2005.

ANSWERS TO TEST YOUR UNDERSTANDINGS 1 and 2

1: a. LIST 200   b. LIST 300-330   c. LIST 300-
2: a. The line number of the last line to be deleted must be specified. It should read

```
DELETE -450
```

b. Nothing wrong.
c. The lower line number must come first. The command should read

```
DELETE 200-300
```

4.7 Some Programming Tips

Writing programs in BASIC is not difficult. However, it does require a certain amount of care and meticulous attention to detail. Each person must develop an individual programming style.

Here are a few tips that may help you over some of the rough spots of writing those first few programs.

Programming Tips

1. Carefully think your program through. Break up the computation into steps. Describe each step in clear English. (If you can't tell yourself what you want the computer to do, it is unlikely that you can tell the computer.)
2. Write a set of instructions corresponding to each step. Check your instructions carefully, with an eagle eye for misspellings, missing parentheses, and other embarrassing gaffes.
3. Pepper your work with remarks. Next week (or next month) you may wish to modify your program. It's embarrassing not to be able to figure out how your own program works!
4. Type your program so that you can read it like a story. (More on how to do this in the next chapter.)
5. Work your program through by hand, pretending that you are the computer. Don't rush. Go through your program one step at a time and check that it does what you want it to do.
6. Have you given all variables the values you want? Remember, if you do not specify the value of a variable, BASIC will automatically assign it the value zero. This may not be the value you intend!

In the upcoming chapters we will not only teach you how to program in BASIC, we will also encourage you to develop good programming habits and a useful programming style. In the process, we will add to the above list of programming tips.

4.8 Using the BASIC Editor

Suppose that you discover a program line with an error in it. How can you correct it? Up to now, the only way was to retype the line. There is a much better way. The IBM Personal Computer has a powerful **editor**. This editor allows you to add, delete, or change text in existing program lines. This section is designed to teach you to use the editor.

The editing process (the process of changing or correcting characters already typed) consists of three steps:

92 Getting Started in BASIC

1. Indicate the location of the change.
2. Input the change.
3. Send the change to the computer via the **ENTER** key.

These steps make use of a number of special editing keys. Most of these keys are found on the numeric keypad. As we told you earlier, the numeric keypad may be used to input numbers just as you would from a calculator keyboard. To use the numeric keypad in this fashion, the **Num Lock** key must be in the engaged position. With the **Num Lock** key disengaged, the keys of the numeric keypad assume the alternate functions indicated on the keys by symbols such as →, ←, ↑, ↓, DEL, and so forth. These alternate functions are used for editing. Note that the **Num Lock** key is in the disengaged position when you first turn on the computer, so the keypad is already set for editing.

The best way to understand the editing process is to work through several examples. If at all possible follow these examples by typing them out on your keyboard. Suppose you have typed the following program lines:

```
10 PRIMT X,Y,Z
20 IF A=5 THN 50 ELSE 30
_
```

The third line indicates the cursor position. We immediately see that there are two spelling errors: PRIMT and THN. (If the computer had any common sense, it would have known what you meant.) In addition, suppose that we wish to change X, Y, and Z in the first line to read A, X, Y, Z. Finally, suppose we wish to delete the ELSE 30 on the second line. Let's use the editing process to correct them. The first step is to position the cursor at the first character to be corrected. To do this we use various keys on the numeric keypad that move the cursor like this:

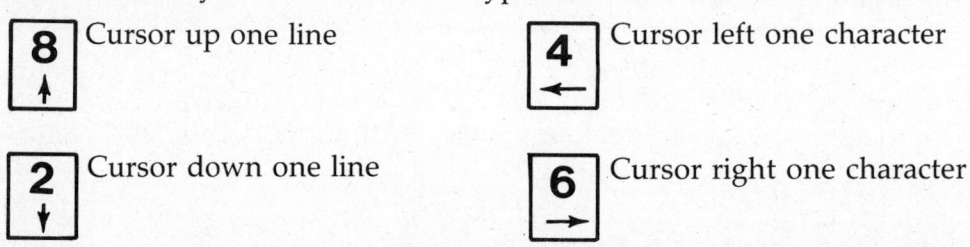

| **8** ↑ | Cursor up one line | **4** ← | Cursor left one character |
| **2** ↓ | Cursor down one line | **6** → | Cursor right one character |

(There are other cursor motion keys, but let's study only these for now.) To correct the PRIMT error we must first position the cursor at the M. To do this we first hit the ↑ key twice. This moves the cursor up two lines. The display now looks like this:

```
10 PRIMT X,Y,Z
20 IF A=5 THN 50 ELSE 30
```

Next we hit the → key six times to move the cursor to the right six spaces. (Note that the space between 0 and P counts.) The display now looks like this:

```
10 PRIMT X,Y,Z
20 IF A=5 THN 50 ELSE 30
```

We have now accomplished step 1: The cursor is at the character to be corrected. Now we execute step 2: We type in the change. In this case, we type N. Note that the N replaces the M. Here is the display:

```
10 PRINT X,Y,Z
20 IF A=5 THN 50 ELSE 30
```

The first error has now been corrected. Note, however, that the correction has not yet been sent to the computer via the **ENTER** key. We could do so at this point, but it wouldn't make much sense since there is another error to correct on the same line. Let's tend to that error now. To do so, we must insert the characters A and , before the X. Move the cursor two spaces to the right. Here is the display:

```
10 PRINT X,Y,Z
20 IF A=5 THN 50 ELSE 30
```

To insert text at the cursor position, we hit the **Ins** key and type the material to be inserted: A,. The **Ins** key puts the computer in **insert mode**. In this mode, typed text is inserted at the current position and all other text moves to the right. Here is the current display:

```
10 PRINT A,X,Y,Z
20 IF A=5 THN 50 ELSE 30
```

Since we have finished the insertion, we cancel the insert mode. This may be done in several ways. One method is to hit the Ins key again. This would allow us to continue to make further corrections on the same line. Another method (in this case the preferred one) is to hit the ENTER key. This cancels the insert mode and sends the corrected line to the computer. Note that the cursor may be in any position on the line when the ENTER command is given. Here is the display after ENTER.

```
10 PRINT A,X,Y,Z
20 IF A=5 THN 50 ELSE 30
```

Note that the cursor is now at the first character of line 20. We correct the misspelling of THEN by moving the cursor to the N (14 spaces to the right), typing **Ins** followed by E, followed by **Ins**. Here is how the display looks now.

```
10 PRINT A,X,Y,Z
20 IF A = 5 THEN 50 ELSE 30
```

The final correction is to delete ELSE 30. This is done using the **Del** key. First we position the cursor on the E in ELSE. Then we hit the **Del** key seven times. Each repetition of the **Del** key deletes the character at the

94 Getting Started in BASIC

current cursor position and moves the remaining text to the left. For example, after hitting **Del** the first time, the display looks like this

```
10 PRINT A,X,Y,Z
20 IF A=5 THEN 50 LSE 30
```

After seven repetitions of the Del key, the display looks like this

```
10 PRINT A,X,Y,Z
20 IF A=5 THEN 50 _
```

The corrections are now complete. We send the line to the computer via the **ENTER** key.

The above example illustrates various editing features of the IBM Personal Computer. We may use the editing keys in the same way, to alter any line on the screen. If you wish to alter a program line that is not currently on the screen, you may display the desired line using the **LIST** command. Editing would then take place as shown.

There are a number of other keys that make editing faster. For example, to speed up cursor movement, we have the following keys:

Home. This key moves the cursor to the upper left corner of the screen (the so-called "home" position).

Ctrl Home. This key combination clears the screen and brings the cursor to the home position.

Ctrl →. This key combination moves the cursor to the space right of the beginning of the next word. (Think of a word as any sequence of characters not containing spaces. This is not exactly correct, but is close enough for practical purposes.)

Ctrl ←. This key combination moves the cursor to the space left of the beginning of the next word.

End. This key moves the cursor to the end of the current line.

In addition to the editing keys described above, the following two key combinations are useful.

Ctrl End. This key combination erases input from the current cursor position to the end of the line.

Ctrl Break. This key combination cancels all editing changes in the current line.

IMPORTANT NOTE:

Editing changes occur only in the copy of the program in RAM. In order for changes to be reflected in copies of the program on cassette or diskette, it is necessary to save the edited copy of the program. The moral:

AFTER MAKING CORRECTIONS, SAVE YOUR PROGRAM!

4.8 Using the BASIC Editor

Exercises

What keystrokes accomplish the following editing functions?
1. Move the cursor four spaces to the right.
2. Delete the fourth letter to the right of the cursor.
3. Insert the characters 538 at the current cursor position.
4. Delete the portion of the line to the right of the cursor position.
5. Move the cursor up eight spaces.
6. Move the cursor to the right three spaces.
7. List the current version of the line.
8. Change 0 to a 1 at the current cursor position.
9. Delete the letter "a" eight spaces to the left of the current cursor position.
10. Cancel all changes in the current line.

Use the line editor to make the indicated changes in the following program line. The exercises are to be done in order.

```
300 FOR M = 11 TO 99, SETP .5 : X = M^2 - 5
```

11. Delete the comma (,).
12. Correct the misspelling of the word STEP.
13. Change $M^2 - 5$ to $M^3 - 2$.
14. Change .5 to -1.5.
15. Add the following characters to the end of the line: Y=M+1.

Controlling the Flow of Your Program

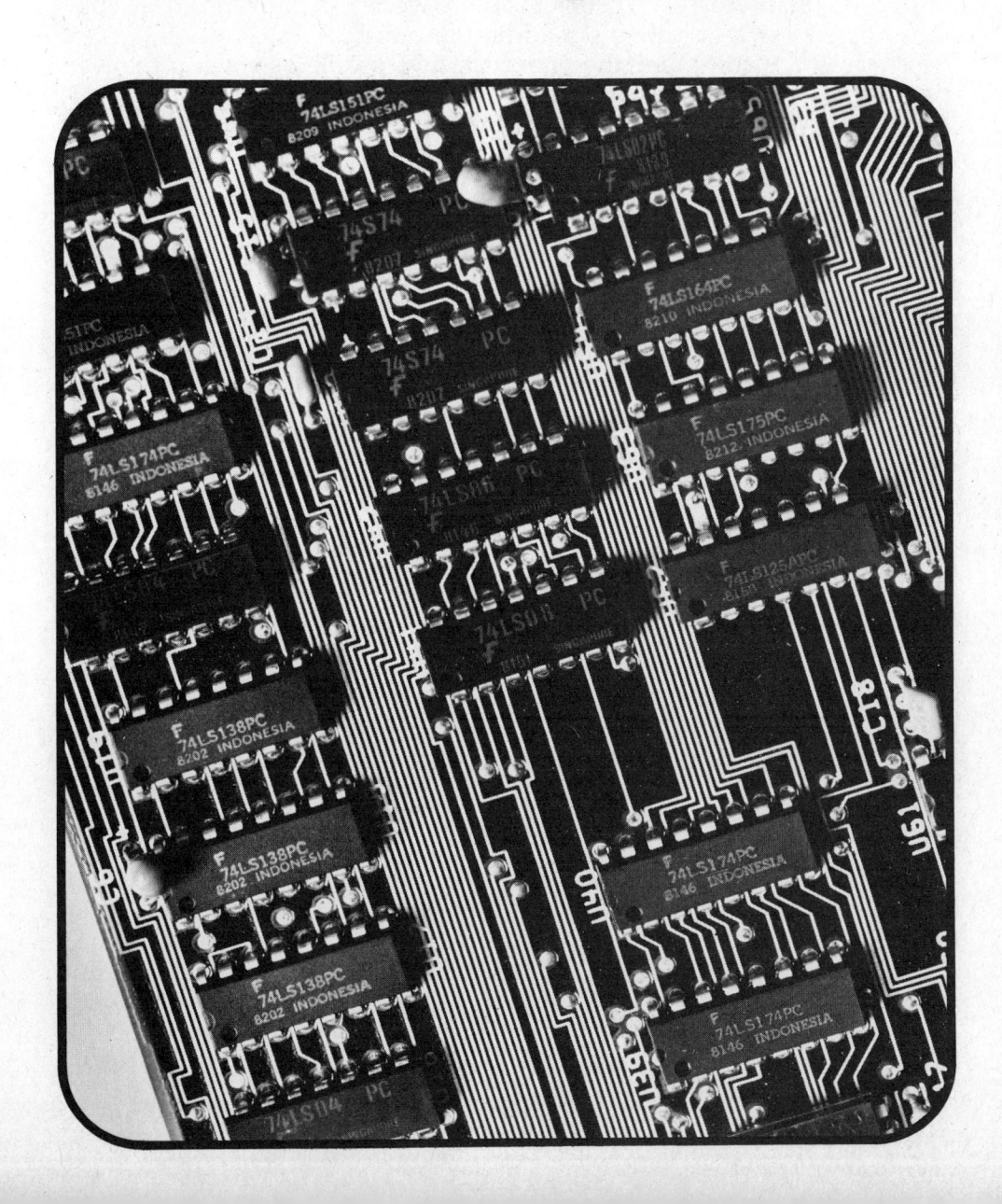

5

98   Controlling the Flow of Your Program

In this chapter we will continue our introduction of diskette BASIC on the IBM Personal Computer. Our discussion will center on the instructions for controlling the flow of statement execution.

5.1 Doing Repetitive Operations

Suppose that we wish to solve 50 similar multiplication problems. It is certainly possible to type in the 50 problems one at a time and let the computer solve them. However, this is a very clumsy way to proceed. Suppose that instead of 50 problems there were 500 or even 5000. Typing the problems one at a time would not be practical. If, however, we can describe to the computer the entire class of problems we want solved, then we can instruct the computer to solve them using only a few BASIC statements. Let us consider a concrete problem. Suppose that we wish to calculate the quantities

$$1^2, 2^2, 3^2, \ldots, 10^2$$

That is, we wish to calculate a table of squares of integers from 1 to 10. This calculation can be described to the computer as calculating N^2, where the variable N is allowed to assume, one at a time, each of the values 1, 2, 3, ...,10. Here is a sequence of BASIC statements that accomplish the calculations:

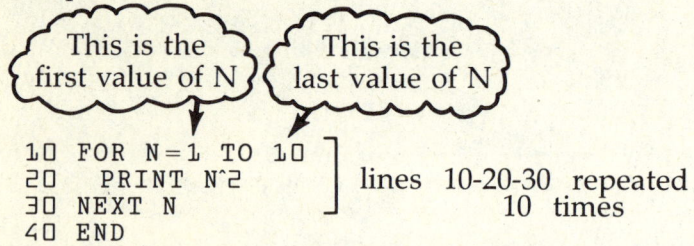

```
10 FOR N=1 TO 10
20    PRINT N^2         lines 10-20-30 repeated
30 NEXT N                      10 times
40 END
```

(This is the first value of N) (This is the last value of N)

The sequence of statements 10,20,30 is called a **loop**. When the computer encounters the **FOR** statement, it sets N equal to 1 and continues executing the statements. Line 20 calls for printing N^2. Since N is equal to 1, we have N^2=1^2=1. So the computer will print a 1. Next comes statement 30, which calls for the next N. This instructs the computer to return to the **FOR** statement in 10, increase N to 2, and to repeat instructions 20 and 30. This time N^2=2^2=4. Line 20 then prints a 4. Line 30 says to go back to line 10 and increase N to 3 and so forth. Lines 10, 20, and 30 are repeated 10 times! After the computer executes lines 10, 20, and 30 with N = 10, it will leave the loop and execute line 40.

Type in the above program and give the **RUN** command. The output will look like this:

```
1
4
9
```

```
16
25
36
49
64
81
100
Ok
```

The variable N is called the **loop variable**. It may be used inside the loop just like any other variable. For example, it may be used in algebraic calculations and PRINT statements.

> **TEST YOUR UNDERSTANDING 1 (answers on page 108)**
> a. Devise a loop allowing N to assume the values 3 to 77.
> b. Write a program which calculates N^2 for $N = 3$ to 77.

Making Loops More Readable

Note that we have indented the text portion of line 20. This allows us to clearly see the beginning and end of the loop. It is good programming practice to always indent loops in this way since it increases program readability. The TAB key (the key with the two symbols →| and |←) may be used to indent. BASIC sets up tab stops every five spaces. These are just like the tab stops on a typewriter. Whenever you press the Tab key, the cursor moves over to the next tab stop.

Let's modify the above program to include on each line of output not only N^2, but also the value of N. To make the table easier to read, let's also add two column headings. The new program reads:

```
10 PRINT "N","N^2"
20 FOR N=1 TO 10
30    PRINT N,N^2
40 NEXT N
50 END
```

The output now looks like this:

```
N            N^2
1            1
2            4
3            9
4            16
5            25
6            36
7            49
8            64
9            81
10           100
Ok
```

100 Controlling the Flow of Your Program

> **TEST YOUR UNDERSTANDING 2 (answer on page 108)**
>
> What would happen if we change the number of line 10 to 25?

Let us now illustrate some of the many uses loops have by means of some examples.

Example 1. Write a BASIC program to calculate $1+2+3+\ldots+100$.

Solution. Let us use a variable S (for sum) to contain the sum. Let us start S at 0 and use a loop to successively add to S the numbers 1, 2, 3, ..., 100. Here is the program.

```
10 LET S=0
20 FOR N=1 TO 100  ⎫
30   LET S=S + N    ⎬  These instructions
40 NEXT N          ⎭  repeated 100 times
50 PRINT S
60 END
```

When we enter the loop the first time, $S=0$ and $N=1$. Line 30 then replaces S by $S + N$, or $0 + 1$. Line 40 sends us back to line 20 where the value of N is now set equal to 2. In line 30 S (which is now $0 + 1$) is replaced by $S + N$, or $0 + 1 + 2$. Line 40 now sends us back to line 20, where N is now set equal to 3. Line 30 then sets S equal to $0 + 1 + 2 + 3$. Finally, on the 100th time through the loop, S is replaced by $0 + 1 + 2 + \ldots + 100$, the desired sum. If we run the program, we derive the output

```
5050
Ok
```

> **TEST YOUR UNDERSTANDING 3 (answer on page 108)**
>
> Write a BASIC program to calculate $101+102+\ldots+110$.

> **TEST YOUR UNDERSTANDING 4 (answer on page 108)**
>
> Write a BASIC program to calculate and display the numbers $2, 2^2, 2^3, \ldots, 2^{20}$.

Example 2. Write a program to calculate the sum:

$$1 \times 2 + 2 \times 3 + 3 \times 4 + \ldots + 49 \times 50$$

Solution. We let the sum be contained in the variable S as we did in the preceding example. The quantities to be added are just the numbers $N*(N+1)$ for $N=1, 2, 3, \ldots, 49$. Here is our program:

```
10 LET S=0
20 FOR N=1 TO 49
30    LET S=S + N*(N+1)
40 NEXT N
50 PRINT S
60 END
```

Some Cautions

Here are two of the errors you are most likely to make in dealing with loops.

1. Every FOR statement must have a corresponding NEXT. Otherwise, BASIC will halt your program and display the error message:

    ```
    FOR without NEXT in line xxxxx
    ```

2. Be sure that the loop variable is not already used with some other meaning. For example, suppose that the loop variable N is used before the loop begins. The loop will destroy the old value of N, and there is no way to get it back after the loop is over.

Nested Loops

In many applications it is necessary to execute a loop within a loop. For example, suppose that we wish to compute the following series of numbers:

$1^2, 2^2, 3^2, \ldots, 10^2,$
$101^2, 102^2, 103^2, \ldots, 110^2,$
$\ldots$
$\ldots$
$2001^2, 2002^2, 2003^2, \ldots, 2010^2$

There are 21 groups of 10 numbers each. Each line may be computed using a loop. For example, the first line may be computed using:

```
100 FOR I=1 TO 10
110    PRINT I^2
120 NEXT I
```

The second line may be computed using:

```
100 FOR I=1 TO 10
110    PRINT (100+I)^2
120 NEXT I
```

And the last line may be computed using:

```
100 FOR I=1 TO 10
110    PRINT (2000+I)^2
120 NEXT I
```

102 Controlling the Flow of Your Program

We could compute the desired numbers by repeating essentially the same instructions 21 times. However, it is much easier to do the repetition using a loop. The numbers to be added to I range from 0 (which is 0*100) for the first line, to 100 (which is 1*100) for the second line, to 2000 (which is 20*100) for the last line. This suggests that we represent these numbers as J*100, where J is a loop variable which runs from 0 to 20. We may then compute our desired table of numbers using this program:

```
10   FOR J=0 TO 20
100     FOR I=1 TO 10
110       PRINT (100*J+I)^2
120     NEXT I
200  NEXT J
```

The instructions which are indented one level are repeated 21 times, corresponding to the values J=0 through J=20. On the first repetition (J=0), lines 100-120 print the numbers in the first line; on the second repetition (J=1), lines 100-120 print the numbers in the second line, and so forth. Note how the indentations help to read the program. This is an example of good programming style.

If a loop is contained within a loop, then we say that the loops are **nested**. BASIC allows you to have nesting in as many layers as you wish (a loop within a loop within a loop and so forth.)

TEST YOUR UNDERSTANDING 5 (answer on page 108)

Write a BASIC program to print the following table of numbers.

1	11	21	31
2	12	22	32
.			
.			
.			
9	19	29	39

Warning: Nested loops may not "overlap." That is, the following sequence is not allowed:

```
10  FOR J=1 TO 100
20     FOR K=1 TO 50
.
.
.
80  NEXT J
90     NEXT K
```

Rather, the NEXT K statement must precede the NEXT J, so that the K loop is "completely inside" the J-loop.

Applications of Loops

Example 3. You borrow $7000 to buy a car. You finance the balance for 36 months at an interest rate of one percent per month. Your monthly payments are $232.50. Write a program that computes the amount of interest each month, the amount of the loan which is repaid, and the balance owed.

Solution. Let B denote the balance owed. Initially we have B equal to 7000 dollars. At the end of each month let us compute the interest (I) owed for that month, namely .01*B. For example, at the end of the first month, the interest owed is .01*7000.00 = $70.00. Let P = 232.50 to denote the monthly payment, and let R denote the amount repaid out of the current payment. Then R = P − I. For example, at the end of the first month, the amount of the loan repaid is 232.50 − 70.00 = 162.50. The balance owed may then be calculated as B − R. At the end of the first month, the balance owed is 7000.00 − 162.50 = 6837.50. Here is a program which performs these calculations:

```
10 PRINT "MONTH","INTEREST","PAYMENT","BALANCE"
20 LET B=7000        :'B=initial balance
25 LET P=232.50      :'P=monthly payment
30 FOR M=1 TO 36     :'M is month number
40   LET I=.01*B     :'Calculate interest for month
50   LET R=P - I     :'Calculate repayment
60   LET B=B - R     :'Calculate new balance
70   PRINT M,I,R,B   :'Print out data for month
80 NEXT M
90 END
```

You should attempt to run this program. Notice that it runs, but it is pretty useless because the screen will not contain all of the output. Most of the output goes flying by before you can read it. One method for remedying this situation is to press **Ctrl** and **Num Lock** simultaneously as the output scrolls by on the screen. This will pause execution of the program and freeze the contents of the screen. To resume execution and unfreeze the screen press any key. The output will begin to scroll again. Using this technique requires some manual dexterity. Moreover, it is not possible to guarantee where the scrolling will stop.

> **TEST YOUR UNDERSTANDING 6**
>
> RUN the program of Example 3 and practice freezing the output on the screen. It may take several runs before you are comfortable with the procedure.

Let us now describe another method of adapting the output to our screen size by printing only 12 months of data at one time. This amount of data will fit since the screen contains 24 lines. We will use a second loop to keep track of 12-month periods. The variable for the new loop

Controlling the Flow of Your Program

will be Y (for "years"), and Y will go from 0 to 2. The month variable will be M as before, but now M will go only from 1 to 12. The month number will now be 12*Y + M (12 times the number of years plus the number of months). Here is the revised program.

```
 10 LET B=7000
 20 LET P=232.50
 30 FOR Y=0 TO 2 :        'Y=year number
 40   PRINT "MONTH","INTEREST","PAYMENT","BALANCE"
 50   FOR M=1 TO 12 :'Run through the months of year Y.
 60     LET I=.01*B:       'Calculate interest for month
 70     LET R=P - I:       'Calculate repayment for month
 80     LET B=B - R:       'Calculate balance for month
 90     PRINT 12*Y+M,I,R,B:'Print data for month
100   NEXT M
110   STOP              :' Halts execution
120   CLS               :' Clears Screen
130 NEXT Y              :' Goes to next 12 months
140 END
```

This program utilizes several new statements. In line 110 we use the **STOP** statement. This causes the computer to stop execution of the program. The computer remembers where it stops, however, and all values of the variables are preserved. The **STOP** statement also leaves unchanged the contents of the screen. You can take as long as you wish to examine the data on the screen. When you are ready for the program to continue, type **CONT** and press ENTER. The computer will resume where it left off. The first instruction it encounters is in line 120. **CLS** clears the screen. So, after being told to continue, the computer clears the screen and goes on to the next value of Y—the next 12 months of data. Here is a copy of the output. The underlined statements are those you type.

```
Ok
RUN
MONTH           INTEREST        PAYMENT         BALANCE
 1              70              162.5           6837.5
 2              68.375          164.125         6673.375
 3              66.73375        165.7663        6507.609
 4              65.07609        167.4239        6340.185
 5              63.40185        169.0982        6171.087
 6              61.71086        170.7891        6000.298
 7              60.00297        172.497         5827.8
 8              58.278          174.222         5653.578
 9              56.53578        175.9642        5477.614
10              54.77614        177.7239        5299.89
11              52.9989         179.5011        5120.389
12              51.20389        181.2961        4939.093
```

5.1 Doing Repetitive Operations 105

```
Break in 100
Ok
CONT
```

MONTH	INTEREST	PAYMENT	BALANCE
13	49.39093	183.1091	4755.984
14	47.55984	184.9402	4571.044
15	45.71044	186.7896	4384.255
16	43.84255	188.6575	4195.597
17	41.95597	190.544	4005.053
18	40.05053	192.4495	3812.603
19	38.12603	194.374	3618.229
20	36.18229	196.3177	3421.912
21	34.21912	198.2809	3223.631
22	32.23631	200.2637	3023.367
23	30.23367	202.2663	2821.101
24	28.21101	204.289	2616.812

```
Break in 100
Ok
CONT
```

MONTH	INTEREST	PAYMENT	BALANCE
25	26.16812	206.33219	2410.48
26	24.1048	208.3952	2202.085
27	22.02085	210.4792	1991.606
28	19.91606	212.584	1779.022
29	17.79022	214.7098	1564.312
30	15.64312	216.8569	1347.455
31	13.47455	219.0255	1128.43
32	11.28429	221.2157	907.2138
33	9.072137	223.4279	683.7859
34	6.837859	225.6622	458.1238
35	4.58126	227.9188	230.205
36	2.30205	230.198	7.034302E-03

```
Ok
```

Note that the data in the output is carried out to seven figures even though the problem deals with dollars and cents. We will look at the problem of rounding numbers later. Also note the balance listed at the end of month 36. It is in scientific notation. The -03 indicates that the decimal point is to be moved three places to the left. The number listed is .007034302 or about .70 cents (less than one cent)! The computer shifted to scientific notation since the usual notation (.007034302) requires more than seven digits. The computer made the choice of which form of the number to display.

Using Loops to Create Delays

By using a loop we can create a delay inside the computer. Consider the following sequence of instructions:

```
10 FOR N=1 TO 3000
20 NEXT N
```

106   Controlling the Flow of Your Program

This loop doesn't do anything! However, the computer repeats instructions 10 and 20 three thousand times! This may seem like a lot of work. But not for a computer. To obtain a feel for the speed at which the computer works, you should time this sequence of instructions. Such a loop may be used as a delay. For example, when you wish to keep some data on the screen without stopping the program, just build in a delay. Here is a program that prints two screens of text. A delay is imposed to give a person time to read the first screen.

```
10 PRINT "THIS IS A GRAPHICS PROGRAM TO DISPLAY SALES"
20 PRINT "FOR THE YEAR TO DATE"
30 FOR N=1 TO 5000
40 NEXT N:             } Delay Loop
50 CLS
60 PRINT "YOU MUST SUPPLY THE FOLLOWING PARAMETERS:"
70 PRINT "PRODUCT, TERRITORY, SALESPERSON"
80 END
```

Example 4. Use a loop to produce a blinking display for a security system.

Solution. Suppose that your security system is tied in with your computer and the system detects an intruder in your warehouse. Let us print out the message

```
SECURITY SYSTEM DETECTS INTRUDER-ZONE 2
```

For attention, let us blink this message on and off by alternately printing the message and clearing the screen.

```
10 FOR N=1 TO 2000
20    PRINT "SECURITY SYSTEM DETECTS INTRUDER-ZONE 2"
30    FOR K=1 TO 50
40    NEXT K
50    CLS
60 NEXT N
70 END
```

The loop in lines 30-40 is a delay loop to keep the message on the screen a moment. Line 50 turns the message off, but the **PRINT** statement in line 20 turns it back on. The message will blink 2000 times.

TEST YOUR UNDERSTANDING 7 (answer on page 108)

Write a program that blinks your name on the screen 500 times and leaves your name on the screen for a loop of length 50 each time.

More About Loops

In all of our loop examples, the loop variable increased by one with each repetition of the loop. However, it is possible to have the loop variable change by any amount. For example, the instructions

5.1 Doing Repetitive Operations

```
10 FOR N=1 TO 5000 STEP 2
 .
 .
 .
1000 NEXT N
```

define a loop where N jumps by 2 for each repetition, so N will assume the values:

1,3,5,7,9,...,4999

Similarly, use of STEP .5 in the above loop will cause N to advance by .5 and assume the values:

1, 1.5, 2, 2.5, 3, 3.5, 4, 4.5, ... , 5000

It is even possible to have a negative step. In this case, the loop variable will run backwards. For example, the instructions

```
10 FOR N=100 TO 1 STEP -1
 .
 .
 .
100 NEXT N
```

will "count down" from N=100 to N=1 one unit at a time. We will give some applications of such instructions in the Exercises.

TEST YOUR UNDERSTANDING 8 (answers on page 108)

Write instructions letting N assume the following sequences of values:
   a. 95,96.7,98.4,...,112
   b. 200,199.5,199,...,100

Exercises (answers on page 367)

Write BASIC programs to compute the following quantities.
1. $1^2 + 2^2 + 3^2 + \ldots + 25^2$
2. $(½)^0 + (½)^1 + (½)^2 + \ldots + (½)^{10}$
3. $1^3 + 2^3 + 3^3 + \ldots + 10^3$
4. $1 + (½) + (⅓) + \ldots + (1/100)$
5. Write a program to compute N^2, N^3, and N^4 for N = 1,...,12. The format of your output should be as follows:

```
N      N^2      N^3      N^4

1
2
3
.
.
.
12
```

108   Controlling the Flow of Your Program

6. Suppose that you have a car loan whose current balance is $4,000.00. The monthly payment is $125.33 and the interest is one percent per month on the unpaid balance. Make a table of the interest payments and balances for the next 12 months.
7. Suppose you deposit $1,000 on January 1 of each year into a savings account paying 10 percent interest. Suppose that the interest is computed on January 1 of each year, based on the balance for the preceding year. Calculate the balances in the account for each of the next 15 years.
8. A stock market analyst predicts that Tyro Computers, Inc. will achieve a 20 percent growth in sales in each of the next three years, but profits will grow at a 30 percent annual rate. Last year's sales were $35 million and last year's profits were $5.54 million. Project the sales and profits for the next three years based on the analyst's prediction.

ANSWERS TO TEST YOUR UNDERSTANDINGS 1, 2, 3, 4, 5, and 7

1: a. 10 FOR N = 3 TO 77
        .
        .
       100 NEXT N

   b. 10 FOR N = 3 TO 77
       20   PRINT N^2
       30 NEXT N
       40 END

2: The heading

   N   N^2

   would be printed before each entry of the table.

3: 10 S = 0
   20 FOR N = 101 TO 110
   30   S = S + N
   40 NEXT N
   50 PRINT S
   60 END

4: 10 FOR N = 1 TO 20
   20   PRINT 2^N
   30 NEXT N
   40 END

5: 10 FOR J = 1 TO 9
   20   FOR I = 0 TO 3
   30   PRINT 10*I + J,
   40   NEXT I:PRINT
   50 NEXT J

7: 10 FOR N = 1 TO 500
   20   PRINT "<YOUR NAME>"
   30   FOR K = 1 TO 50
   40   NEXT K

```
      50    CLS
      60    NEXT N
      70    END
   8: a.   10 FOR N=95 TO 112 STEP 1.7
      b.   20 FOR N=200 TO 100 STEP .5
```

5.2 Letting Your Computer Make Decisions

BASIC contains instructions that allow you to ask a question. The computer will determine the answer and will take an action which depends on the answer. Here are some examples of questions that the computer can answer:

IS A GREATER THAN ZERO?
IS A^2 AT LEAST 200?
DOES THE STRING NAME$ BEGIN WITH A "Z" ?
IS AT LEAST ONE OF THE VARIABLES A, B OR C NEGATIVE?

Here are two BASIC statements that allow you to ask such questions: The **IF...THEN** statement and the **IF...THEN...ELSE** statement. The first of these statements has the form:

```
IF <question> THEN <statement or line number>
```

Here is how this statement works:
1. The "question" part of an IF...THEN statement allows you to ask questions like those above.
2. If the answer to the question is YES, the program executes the portion of the statement following THEN.
   a. If a statement follows THEN, this statement is executed.
   b. If a line number follows THEN, the program continues execution with this line number.
3. If the answer to the question is NO, the program continues with the next statement.

For example, consider this instruction:

```
500 IF N=0 THEN PRINT "CALCULATION DONE"
```

The question portion of this instruction is N=0; the portion following THEN is the statement: PRINT "CALCULATION DONE". When the computer encounters this statement, it first determines if N is equal to zero. If so, it prints "CALCULATION DONE" and proceeds with the next instruction after line 500. However, if N is not zero, the program immediately goes to the next instruction line after 500. (It ignores the statement after THEN.)

Here is another example:

```
600 IF A^2 < 1 THEN 300
```

When the program reaches this instruction, it will examine the value of A^2. If A^2 is less than 1, the program will go to line 300. Otherwise, the program will go on to the next instruction.

The IF...THEN...ELSE statement is similar to an IF...THEN statement, except it allows for added flexibility in case the answer to the question is NO. The form of the IF...THEN...ELSE statement is:

```
IF <question> THEN <statement or line number>
     ELSE <statement or line number>
```

This statement works as follows: The computer asks the given question. If the answer is YES, the program executes the THEN portion; if the answer is NO, the program executes the ELSE portion.

Here is an example:

```
500 IF N=0 THEN PRINT "CALCULATION DONE" ELSE 250
```

The computer first determines if N equals 0. If so, it prints CALCULATION DONE. If N is not equal to 0, the program continues execution at line 250.

Another possibility is for both **THEN** and **ELSE** to be followed by instructions, as in this example:

```
600 IF A + B>=100 THEN PRINT A + B ELSE PRINT A
```

In executing this instruction, the computer will determine whether A+B is greater than or equal to 100. If so, it will print the value of A+B; if not, it will print the value of A. In both cases execution continues with the next instruction after line 600.

After **IF**, you may insert any expression which the computer may test for truth or falsity. Here are some examples:

N=0
N>5 (N is greater than 5)
N<12.9 (N is less than 12.9)
N>=0 (N is greater than or equal to 0)
N<=−1 (N is less than or equal to −1)
N >< 0 (N is not equal to 0)
A + B <> C (A + B is not equal to C)
A^2 + B^2 <= C^2 ($A^2 + B^2$ is less than or equal to C^2)
N=0 OR A > B (Either N=0 or A > B or both)
N > M AND I=0 (Both N > M and I=0)

TEST YOUR UNDERSTANDING 1 (answers on page 122)

Write instructions which do the following:
a. If A is less than B, then print the value of A plus B; if not then go to the end.
b. If A^2 + D is at least 5000 then go to line 300; if not go to line 500.
c. If N is larger than the sum of I and K, then set N equal to the sum of I and K; otherwise, let N equal K.

5.2 Letting Your Computer Make Decisions

The **IF...THEN** and **IF...THEN...ELSE** statements may be used to interrupt the normal sequence of executing program lines, based upon the truth or falsity of some condition. In many applications, however, we will want to perform instructions out of the normal sequence, independent of any conditions. For such applications, we may use the **GOTO** instruction. (This is not a typographical error! There is no space between GO and TO.) This instruction has the form

```
GOTO < line number >
```

For example, the instruction

```
1000 GOTO 300
```

will send the computer back to line 300 for its next instruction.

The next few examples illustrate some of the uses of the **IF...THEN**, **IF...THEN...ELSE**, and **GOTO** statements.

Example 1. A lumber supply house has a policy that a credit invoice may not exceed $1,000, including a 10 percent processing fee and 5 percent sales tax. A customer orders 150 2×4 studs at $1.99 each, 30 sheets of plywood at $14.00 each, 300 pounds of nails at $1.14 per pound, and two double hung insulated windows at $187.95 each. Write a program which prepares an invoice and decides whether the order is over the credit limit.

Solution. Let's use the variables A1, A2, A3, and A4 to denote, respectively, the numbers of studs, sheets of plywood, pounds of nails, and windows. Let's use the variables B1, B2, B3, and B4 to denote the unit costs of these four items. The cost of the order is then computed as:

```
A1*B1+A2*B2+A3*B3+A4*B4
```

We add 10 percent of this amount to cover processing and form the sum to obtain the total order. Next, we compute 5 percent of the last amount as tax and add it to the total to obtain the total amount due. Finally, we determine if the total amount due is more than $1,000. If it is, we print out the message: ORDER EXCEEDS $1,000. CREDIT SALE NOT PERMITTED. Here is our program.

```
10  LET A1=150:A2=30:A3=300:A4=2:      'Assign quantities
20  LET B1=1.99:B2=14:B3=1.14:         'Assign prices
    B4=187.95:
30  LET T=A1*B1+A2*B2+A3*B3+A4*B4:     'T=total price
40  PRINT "TOTAL ORDER",T
50  LET P=.1*T:                        'P=processing fee
60  PRINT "PROCESSING FEE";P
70  LET TX=.05*(P+T):                  'TX=tax
80  PRINT "SALES TAX",TX
90  DU=T + P + TX:                     'DU=Amount due
100 PRINT "AMOUNT DUE", DU
110 IF DU > 1000 THEN 200 ELSE 300:    'Order > $1000 ?
200 PRINT "ORDER EXCEEDS $1,000"
210 PRINT "CREDIT SALE NOT PERMITTED"
```

Controlling the Flow of Your Program

```
220 GOTO 400:                          'End program
300 PRINT "CREDIT SALE OK"
400 END
```

Note the decision in line 110. If the amount due exceeds $1,000 the computer goes to line 200 where it prints out a message denying credit. In line 220, the computer is sent to line 400 which is the END of the program. On the other hand, if the amount due is less than $1,000, the computer is sent to line 300, where credit is approved.

TEST YOUR UNDERSTANDING 2 (answer on page 122)

Suppose that a credit card charges 1.5 percent per month on any unpaid balance up to $500 and 1 percent per month on any excess over $500.
 a. Write a program that computes the service charge and the new balance.
 b. Test your program on the unpaid balances of $1300 and $275.

TEST YOUR UNDERSTANDING 3 (answer on page 122)

Consider the following sequence of instructions.

```
100 IF A>=5 THEN 200
110 IF A>=4 THEN 300
120 IF A>=3 THEN 400
130 IF A>=2 THEN 500
```

Suppose that the current value of A is 3. List the sequence of line numbers that will be executed.

Example 2. At $20 per square yard, a family can afford up to 500 square feet of carpet for their dining room. They wish to install the carpet in a circular shape. It has been decided that the radius of the carpet is to be a whole number of feet. What is the radius of the largest carpet they can afford? (The area of a circle of radius "R" is PI times R^2, where PI equals approximately 3.14159.)

Solution. Let us compute the area of the circle of radius 1,2,3,4,. . . and determine which of the areas are less than 500.

```
10 PI=3.14159
20 R=1 :                               ' R=radius
30 A=PI*R^2 :                          ' A=area
40 'Is A>=500 ? If so, END. Otherwise, PRINT R .
50 IF A >=500 THEN 100 ELSE PRINT R
60 LET R=R + 1 :                       ' Go to next radius
70 GOTO 30:                            ' Repeat
100 END
```

5.2 Letting Your Computer Make Decisions

Note that line 50 contains an **IF...THEN** statement. If A, as computed in line 30, is 500 or more, then the computer goes to line 100, **END**. If A is less than 500, the computer proceeds to the next line, namely 60. It then prints out the current radius, increases the radius by 1, and goes back to line 30 to repeat the entire procedure. Note that lines 30-40-50-60-70 are repeated until the area becomes at least 500. In effect, this sequence of five instructions forms a loop. However, we did not use a **FOR...NEXT** instruction because we did not know in advance how many times we wanted to execute the loop. We let the computer decide the stopping point via the **IF...THEN** instruction.

In Section 1 of this chapter, we discussed the notion of a loop. In this section, we have discussed decision-making. The **WHILE...WEND** pair of statements combine both of the procedures. This statement pair has the form:

```
WHILE <expression>
 .
 .
 .
WEND
```

The statements in between WHILE and WEND are repeated so long as <expression> is true. Note, however, that the statements in between WHILE and WEND may never be executed. If <expression> is initially false, the program skips to the next statement after WEND. The WHILE...WEND pair is useful in executing loops when you cannot specify in advance the number of repetitions.

Example 3. Rewrite the program of Example 2 using the WHILE...WEND pair of statements.

Solution. Here is the program adaptation.

```
10 PI=3.14159
20 R=1 :                    ' R=radius
30 WHILE A<500
40     A=PI*R^2 :            ' A=area
50     PRINT R
60     R=R + 1 :              ' Go to next radius
70 WEND:                     ' Repeat
100 END
```

Example 4. A school board race involves two candidates. The returns from the four wards of the town are as follows:

	Ward 1	Ward 2	Ward 3	Ward 4
Mr. Thompson	487	229	1540	1211
Ms. Wilson	1870	438	110	597

Calculate the total number of votes achieved by each candidate, the percentage achieved by each candidate, and decide who won the election.

Solution. Let A1, A2, A3, and A4 be the totals for Mr. Thompson in the four wards; let B1-B4 be the corresponding numbers for Ms. Wilson. Let TA and TB denote the total votes, respectively, for Mr. Thompson and Ms. Wilson. Here is our program:

```
10  A1=487: A2=229: A3=1540: A4=1211
20  B1=1870: B2=438: B3=110: B4=597
30  TA=A1+A2+A3+A4 :          'Total for Thompson
40  TB=B1+B2+B3+B4 :          'Total for Wilson
50  T=TA + TB :               'Total Votes Cast
60  PA=100*TA/T :             'Percentage for Thompson
70  ' TA/T is the ratio of votes for Thompson.
80  ' Multiply by 100 to convert to a percentage.
90  PB=100*TB/T :             'Percentage for Wilson
100 A$="THOMPSON"
110 B$="WILSON"
120 ' Lines 130-150 print the percentages of the can-
    didates
130 PRINT "CANDIDATE","VOTES","PERCENTAGE"
140 PRINT A$,TA,PA
150 PRINT B$,TB,PB
160 ' Lines 170-400 decide the winner.
170 IF TA>TB THEN 300:        'Thompson wins
180 IF TA<TB THEN 400:        'Wilson wins
190 PRINT A$, "AND", B$, "ARE TIED!": 'Otherwise a tie
200 GOTO 1000:                'End
300 PRINT A$, "WINS"
310 GOTO 1000                 'End
400 PRINT B$, "WINS"
1000 END
```

Note the logic used for deciding who won. In line 170 we compare the votes TA and TB. If TA is the larger, then A (Thompson) is the winner. We then go to 300, print the result, and END. On the other hand, if TA > TB is *false*, then either B wins or the two are tied. According to the program, if TA > TB is false, we go to line 180, where we determine if TA < TB. If this is true, then B is the winner, we go to 400, print the result, and END. On the other hand, if TA < TB is false, then the only possibility left is that TA = TB. According to the program, if TA = TB we go to 200, where we print the proper result, and then END.

Infinite Loops and Ctrl-Break

As we have seen above, it is very convenient to be able to execute a loop without knowing in advance how many times the loop will be executed. However, with this convenience comes a danger. It is possible to create a loop that will be repeated an infinite number of times! For example, consider the following program:

```
10 LET N=1
20 PRINT N
30 LET N=N+1
```

```
40 GOTO 20
50 END
```

The variable N starts off at 1. We print it and then increase N by 1 (to 2), print it, increase N by 1 (to 3), print it, and so forth. This program will go on forever! Such programs should clearly be avoided. However, even experienced programmers occasionally create infinite loops. When this happens, there is no need to panic. There is a way of stopping the computer. Just press the **Ctrl** and **Break** keys simultaneously. (In the following we will refer to this key comination of keys as **Ctrl-Break**.) This key sequence will interrupt the program currently in progress and return the computer to the command mode. The computer is then ready to accept a command from the keyboard. Note, however, that any program in RAM is undisturbed.

TEST YOUR UNDERSTANDING 4

Type the above program, RUN it, and stop it using the Break key. After stopping it, RUN the program again.

The INPUT Statement

It is very convenient to have the computer request information from you while the program is actually running. This can be accomplished via the **INPUT** statement. To see how, consider the statement

```
570 INPUT A
```

When the computer encounters this statement in the course of executing the program, it displays a **?** and waits for you to respond by typing the desired value of A (and then hitting the **ENTER** key). The computer then sets A equal to the numeric value you specified and continues running the program.

You may use an **INPUT** statement to specify the values of several different variables at one time. These variables may be numeric or string variables. For example, suppose that the computer encounters the statement

```
50 INPUT A,B,C$
```

It will display

?

You then type in the desired values for A, B, and C$ in the same order as in the program, and separate them by commas. For example, suppose that you type

```
10.5, 11.42, BEARINGS
```

followed by an **ENTER**. The computer will then set

116 Controlling the Flow of Your Program

```
A=10.5, B=11.42, C$="BEARINGS"
```

If you respond to the above question mark by typing only a single number, 10.5, for example, the computer will respond with

```
? Redo from start
?
```

to indicate that you should repeat the input from the beginning. If you attempt to specify a string constant where you should have a numeric constant, the computer will respond with the message

```
? Redo from start
?
```

and will wait for you to repeat the **INPUT** operation.

It is helpful to include a prompting message that describes the input the computer is expecting. To do so, just put the message in quotation marks after the word **INPUT** and place a semicolon after the message (before the list of variables to be input). For example, consider the statement

```
175 INPUT "ENTER COMPANY, AMOUNT"; A$, B
```

When the computer encounters this program line, the dialog will be as follows:

```
ENTER COMPANY, AMOUNT? AJAX OFFICE SUPPLIES, 2579.48
```

The underlined portion indicates your response to the prompt. The computer will now assign these values:

```
A$="AJAX OFFICE SUPPLIES", B=2579.48
```

TEST YOUR UNDERSTANDING 5 (answer on page 122)

Write a program that allows you to set variables A and B to any desired values via an **INPUT** statement. Use the program to set A equal to 12 and B equal to 17.

The next two examples illustrate the use of the **INPUT** statement, and provide further practice in using the **IF. . .THEN** statement.

Example 5. You are a teacher compiling semester grades. Suppose there are four grades for each student and that each grade is on the traditional 0 to 100 scale. Write a program that accepts the grades as input, computes the semester average, and assigns grades according to the following scale:

```
90-100    A
80-89.9   B
70-79.9   C
60-69.9   D
< 60      F
```

5.2 Letting Your Computer Make Decisions 117

Solution. We will use an **INPUT** statement to enter the grades into the computer. Our program will allow you to compute the grades of the students, one after the other, via a loop. You may terminate the loop by entering a negative grade. Here is our program.

```
10 PRINT "ENTER STUDENT'S 4 GRADES."
20 PRINT "SEPARATE GRADES BY COMMAS."
30 PRINT "FOLLOW LAST GRADE WITH ENTER."
40 PRINT "TO END PROGRAM, INCLUDE NEGATIVE GRADE."
50 INPUT A1,A2,A3,A4
60 IF A1<0 THEN 400
70 IF A2<0 THEN 400
80 IF A3<0 THEN 400
90 IF A4<0 THEN 400
100 LET A=(A1+A2+A3+A4)/4
110 PRINT "SEMESTER AVERAGE", A
120 IF A>=90 THEN PRINT "SEMESTER GRADE=A" ELSE 140
130 GOTO 10
140 IF A>=80 THEN PRINT "SEMESTER GRADE=B" ELSE 160
150 GOTO 10
160 IF A>=70 THEN PRINT "SEMESTER GRADE=C" ELSE 180
170 GOTO 10
180 IF A>=60 THEN PRINT "SEMESTER GRADE=D" ELSE 200
190 GOTO 10
200 PRINT "SEMESTER GRADE=F"
300 GOTO 10
400 END
```

Note the logic for printing out the semester grades. First compute the semester average A. In line 120 we ask if A is greater than or equal to 90. If so, we assign the grade A, and go on to the next line, 130, which sends us to line 10 to obtain the next grade. If A is less than 90, line 120 sends us to line 140. In line 140, we ask if A is greater than or equal to 80. If so, then we assign the grade B. (The point is that the only way we can get to line 140 is for A to be less than 90. So if A is greater than or equal to 80, we know that A lies in the B range.) If not, we go to line 160, and so forth. This logic may seem a trifle confusing at first, but after repeated use, it will seem quite natural.

Example 6. Write a program to maintain your checkbook. The program should allow you to record an initial balance, enter deposits, and enter checks. It should also warn you of overdrafts.

Solution. Let the variable B always contain the current balance in the checkbook. The program will ask for the type of transaction you wish to record. A "D" will mean that you wish to record a deposit; a "C" will mean that you wish to record a check; a "Q" will mean that you are done entering transactions and wish to terminate the program. After entering each transaction, the computer will figure your new balance, report it to you, will check for an overdraft, and report any overdraft to you. In case of an overdraft, the program will allow you to cancel the preceding check!

118 Controlling the Flow of Your Program

```
10 INPUT "WHAT IS YOUR STARTING BALANCE"; B
20 INPUT "WHAT TRANSACTION TYPE (D,C,or Q)"; A$
30 IF A$="Q" THEN 1000:      'End
40 IF A$="D" THEN 100 ELSE 200
100 'Process Deposit
110 INPUT "DEPOSIT AMOUNT"; D
120 LET B=B + D :            ' Add desposit to balance
130 PRINT "YOUR NEW BALANCE IS", B
130 GOTO 20
200 'Process check
210 INPUT "CHECK AMOUNT"; C
220 LET B=B - C :            'Deduct check amount
230 IF B<0 THEN 300 :        'Test for overdraft
240 PRINT "YOUR NEW BALANCE IS", B
250 GOTO 20
300 'Process overdraft
310 PRINT "LAST CHECK CAUSES OVERDRAFT"
320 INPUT "DO YOU WISH TO CANCEL CHECK(Y/N)"; E$
330 IF E$="Y" THEN 400
340 PRINT "YOUR NEW BALANCE IS", B
350 GOTO 20
400 'Cancel check
410 LET B=B + C:             'Cancel last check
420 GOTO 20
1000 END
```

You should scan this program carefully to make sure you understand how each of the **INPUT** and **IF. . .THEN** statements are used. In addition, you should use this program to obtain a feel for the dialog between you and your computer when **INPUT** statements are used.

Note how the above program is divided into sections. For visual purposes, each section begins with a line number that is a multiple of 100. Moreover, each section begins with a comment that identifies the function of the section. In order to write a complex program, you should break the program into manageable sections. Don't get caught in a maze of complexity. Work out one section at a time and carefully comment on each section, then put the various sections together into one program.

Example 7. Write a BASIC program that tests mastery in the addition of two-digit numbers. Let the user suggest the problems, and let the program keep score of the number correct out of ten.

Solution. Let us request that the program user suggest pairs of numbers via an **INPUT** statement. The sum will also be requested via an **INPUT** statement. An **IF. . .THEN** statement will be used to judge the correctness. The variable R will keep track of the number correct. We will use a loop to repeat the process ten times.

```
10 FOR N=1 TO 10 :           'Loop to give 10 problems
20    INPUT "TYPE TWO 2-DIGIT NUMBERS"; A,B
30    INPUT "WHAT IS THEIR SUM"; C
40    IF A + B=C THEN 200
100    'Respond to incorrect answer
110    PRINT "SORRY. THE CORRECT ANSWER IS",A+B
```

5.2 Letting Your Computer Make Decisions 119

```
120     GO TO 300 :            'Go to the next problem
200     'Respond to correct answer
210     PRINT "YOUR ANSWER IS CORRECT! CONGRATULATIONS"
220     LET R=R+1 :            'Increase score by 1
300 NEXT N
400 'Print score for 10 problems
410 PRINT "YOUR SCORE IS",R,"CORRECT OUT OF 10"
510 PRINT "TO TRY AGAIN, TYPE RUN"
600 END
```

More About INPUTting Data

The INPUT statement, as we have seen, may be used to input one or more constants (string or numeric) to a running program. However, the INPUT statement has a serious defect. To explain this defect, consider the following statement:

```
10 INPUT A$,B$
```

Suppose that you wish to set A$ equal to the string

```
"Washington,George"
```

and B$ to the string

```
"Jefferson,Thomas"
```

Suppose that you respond to the INPUT prompt by typing

```
Washington,George, Jefferson,Thomas
```

BASIC will report an error:

```
? Redo from start
```

Here is the reason. INPUT looks for commas to separate the data items. The first comma occurs between "Washington" and "George". So INPUT assigns A$ the string "Washington" and B$ the string "George". But this gives excess data so BASIC declares an error. There's a simple way around this. Whenever you wish to INPUT data containing a comma, surround the appropriate strings with quotation marks. In our example, the response

```
"Washington,George","Jefferson,Thomas"
```

will assign A$ and B$ as we wished.

It is something of a bother to surround strings in quotation marks, so BASIC provides another statement that is not sensitive to commas, namely LINE INPUT. The LINE INPUT statement may be used to assign only one variable at a time. It reads the input until it encounters ENTER. For example, suppose that we use the statement

```
30 LINE INPUT A$
```

The computer waits for a response. Suppose that we respond with the string

```
Washington,George
```

and press ENTER. LINE INPUT will then assign A$ the string constant "Washington,George". LINE INPUT may be used only to input data to a string variable.

You may use a prompt with LINE INPUT exactly as you do with INPUT. For example, the statement

```
40 LINE INPUT "Type NAME?";A$
```

Will result in the prompt

```
Type NAME?
```

to which you would respond. Note that LINE INPUT does not automatically display a question mark like the INPUT statement. In the above example the question mark came from the prompt.

There is a third statement that you may use to input data from the keyboard, namely INPUT$. This statement allows you to specify an input of only a specified length. For example, consider the statement

```
10 A$=INPUT$(5)
```

It will cause the program to wait for five characters from the keyboard and will assign them to A$. For example, if you type GEORGE, A$ will be assigned the string constant "GEORG". INPUT$ is a more specialized statement than either INPUT or LINE INPUT because of the following facts:

1. INPUT$ does not automatically display the input characters on the screen. If you want them displayed, it is your responsibility to display them.
2. INPUT$ accepts all keyboard characters, including Backspace and ENTER. In particular, it does not allow you to correct your input.

If you are a beginning programmer, it's probably wisest to stick to INPUT and LINE INPUT, but we mention INPUT$ mainly for completeness.

Exercises (answers on page 368)

1. Write a program to calculate all perfect squares that are less than 45,000. (Perfect squares are the numbers 1,4,9,16,25,36,49,. . . .)
2. Write a program to determine all of the circles of integer radius and area less than or equal to 5,000 square feet. (The area of a circle of radius R is PI*R^2, where PI=3.14159, approximately.)
3. Write a program to determine the sizes of all those boxes that are perfect cubes, have integer dimensions, and have volumes of less than 175,000 cubic feet. (That is, find all integers X where X^3 is less than 175,000.)

4. Modify the arithmetic testing program of Example 7 so that the operation tested is multiplication instead of addition.
5. Modify the arithmetic testing program of Example 7 so that it allows you to choose, at the beginning of each group of ten problems, from among these operations: addition, subtraction, or multiplication.
6. Write a program that accepts three numbers via an INPUT statement and determines the largest of the three.
7. Write a program that accepts three numbers via an INPUT statement and determines the smallest of the three.
8. Write a program that accepts a set of numbers via INPUT statements and determines the largest among them.
9. Write a program that accepts a set of numbers via INPUT statements and determines the smallest among them.
10. The following data were collected by a sociologist. Six cities experienced the following numbers of burglaries in 1980 and 1981:

City	Burglaries 1980	Burglaries 1981
A	5,782	6,548
B	4,811	6,129
C	3,865	4,270
D	7,950	8,137
E	4,781	4,248
F	6,598	7,048

For each city calculate the increase (decrease) in the number of burglaries. Determine which had an increase of more than 500 burglaries.
11. Write a program that does the arithmetic of a cash register. That is, let the program accept purchases via INPUT statements, then total the purchases, figure out the sales tax (assume 5 percent), and compute the total purchase. Let the program ask for the amount of payment given and then let it compute the change due.
12. Write a program that analyzes cash flow. Let the program ask for cash on hand as well as accounts expected to be received in the next month. Let the program also compute the total anticipated cash for the month. Let the program ask for the bills due in the next month, and let it compute the total accounts payable during the month. By comparing the amounts to be received and to be paid out, let the program compute the net cash flow for the month.

> **ANSWERS TO TEST YOUR UNDERSTANDINGS 1, 2, 3, and 5**
>
> 1: a. IF A<B THEN PRINT A+B ELSE END
>   b. IF A^2+D>=5000 THEN 300 ELSE 500
>   c. IF N>I+K THEN N=I+K ELSE N=K
> 2: 10 B =<Your Balance>
>   20 IF B<=500 THEN 200
>   100 LET C=B-500
>   110 IN=.015*500 + .01*C
>   120 GOTO 300
>   200 IN=.015*B
>   300 PRINT "INTEREST EQUALS";IN
>   310 PRINT "NEW BALANCE EQUALS";B+IN
>   320 END
> 3: 100-110-120-400
> 5: 10 INPUT "THE VALUES OF A AND B ARE";A,B
>   20 END

5.3 Structuring Solutions to Problems

You may have noticed our programs getting longer. There is no way around this. In order to utilize the computer to solve real-life problems, programs must often be quite long and must utilize the full range of capabilities of the computer. This poses a number of problems:

1. Long programs are difficult to plan.
2. Long programs are difficult to write and correct.
3. Long programs are hard to read.

All three problems will confront you in programming your computer. Let's discuss some ways to deal with them.

As an example of program planning, let's take the last program of the preceding section. Recall that this is the program that tests addition. Suppose that you are given the job of building such a program. How should you proceed? Your first inclination might be to start writing BASIC statements. At all costs, resist the temptation! Your first job is to plan the program.

The first step in program planning is to decide on the input and output. What data does the user give and what responses does the computer give. Make a list:

User input: Answers to questions
Computer output: Questions to answer
                    Responses to answers
                        a. Response to correct answer
                        b. Response to incorrect answer
                        c. Report of Score
                              Question: Another set of problems?

5.3 Structuring Solutions to Problems

The next step is to organize these inputs and outputs into a sequence of steps that follow one another in logical order. Don't worry about computer instructions at this point. Rather, reasonably describe general steps which, in the end, may actually correspond to several computer instructions. Here is how our addition program might be described.

1. Computer requests question
2. User responds
3. User enters answer
4. Computer analyzes answer and responds
    a. Reports whether answer is correct
    b. Keeps score
5. Steps 1-4 are repeated 10 times
6. Computer reports score
7. Computer queries user whether to begin again.

The third step of program planning is to sketch out the structure of the program. We see from step 5 that we will need a loop to keep track of the problems. Moreover, we know that steps 1-3 are one-line computer commands. Let's lump them together into one section of the program. On the other hand, handling correct answers is different from handling wrong answers. Let's have a separate section of the program for each of these tasks. Moreover, let's have a separate section of the program for steps 6 and 7. You should write all this down (on paper) as follows:

```
10 FOR N=1 TO 10
```

(lines 20-80 reserved for steps 1 to 3.)

```
100   'Respond to incorrect answer
200   'Respond to correct answer
300 NEXT N
400 'Print score for 10 problems
500 'Run again?
600 END
```

At the fourth step you should begin to fill in the various steps in the above outline. Here is where you may begin writing BASIC instructions, defining variables, and so forth. Each of the steps corresponds to only a few program statements. The program then becomes easy to write and our final product is something like the following program.

```
10 FOR N=1 TO 10 :          'Loop to give 10 problems
20    INPUT "TYPE TWO 2-DIGIT NUMBERS"; A,B
30    INPUT "WHAT IS THEIR SUM"; C
40    IF A+B=C THEN 200
100   'Respond to incorrect answer
110   PRINT "SORRY. THE CORRECT ANSWER IS",A+B
120   GO TO 300 :            'Go to the next problem
200   'Respond to correct answer
210   PRINT "YOUR ANSWER IS CORRECT! CONGRATULATIONS"
220   LET R=R+1 :            'Increase score by 1
300 NEXT N:                  'Go to next problem
400 'Print score for 10 problems
```

```
410 PRINT "YOUR SCORE IS",R,"CORRECT OUT OF 10"
500 'Run again?
510 PRINT "TO TRY AGAIN, TYPE RUN"
600 END
```

It is possible that some of the steps correspond to complex sequences of operations. If so, break such steps into smaller steps, just as we have done for the entire program. Eventually, you should reduce your program to an organized sequence of steps, each of which corresponds to no more than about a dozen statements. (The actual number may be more or less, corresponding to your comfort level. Don't allow the number to be too large. This is the way errors creep into your program!)

In organizing a program, you cannot plan the various steps in total isolation from one another. Here are some pitfalls to be aware of:

1. If a variable is to be used in two steps, then it must be given by the same name in each.
2. If a step assumes that the value of a variable has been assigned in a previous step, be sure that this is done.
3. Don't mistakenly use the same variable to mean two different things. This is an easy error to make. After several hours at the keyboard, you may forget that you already used a variable name to mean something else. No harm is done if the two variables are used in two isolated sections of the program. However, you may set the variable with one meaning in mind only to have the program then use it with the other meaning. This can make your results incorrect.
4. Be sure to assign each variable its proper starting value. (This is called **variable initialization**.) Remember that if you do not assign a value to a variable, then BASIC will assign it the value 0.

The procedure for program planning described above automatically incorporates your documentation into your program. This makes it easier to read your program to correct mistakes or to alter it at a later date.

The discussion of this section just scratches the surface of the subject of program planning. Hopefully, it will ease the burden of writing and understanding BASIC programs and will lead you to develop your own approach to program planning and organization. We'll have more to say about the subject in Chapter 7.

5.4 Subroutines

In writing programs it is often necessary to use the same sequence of instructions more than once. It may not be convenient (or even feasible) to retype the set of instructions each time it is needed. Fortunately, BASIC offers a convenient alternative: the subroutine.

A **subroutine** is a program that is incorporated within another, larger program. The subroutine may be used any number of times by the larger program. Often, the lines corresponding to a subroutine are isolated toward the end of the larger program. This arrangement is illustrated in Figure 5-1. The arrow to the subroutine indicates the point in the larger program where the subroutine is used. The arrow pointing away from the subroutine indicates that, after completion of the subroutine, execution of the main program resumes at the point where it was interrupted.

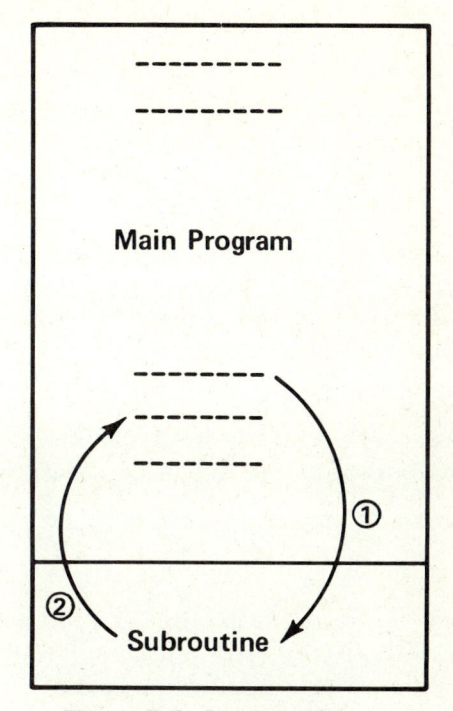

Figure 5-1. A subroutine.

Subroutines are handled with the pair of instructions **GOSUB** and **RETURN**. The statement

```
100 GOSUB 1000
```

sends the computer to the subroutine that begins at line 1000. The computer starts at line 1000 and carries out statements in order. When a **RETURN** statement in the subroutine is reached, the computer goes back to the main program, starting at the first line after 100.

Subroutines may serve as user-defined commands as Example 1 illustrates.

TEST YOUR UNDERSTANDING 1 (answer on page 131)

Consider the following program.

```
10 GOSUB 40
20 PRINT "LINE 20"
30 END
40 PRINT "LINE 40"
50 RETURN
```

List the line numbers in order of execution.

Example 1. Design a BASIC subroutine that erases a specified line on the screen and positions the cursor at the left end of the erased line.

Solution. The task described is required by many programs. It is a prelude to writing on the line. In fact, it may be required many times within the same program. It would be wasteful to write separate instruction lines for each repetition. Let's write a general subroutine that can be called whenever required. Suppose that line L is to be erased. This may be accomplished in the following steps:

1. Position the cursor at the left-most position on the line.
2. Write 80 spaces (40 if you are in WIDTH 40).
3. Reposition the cursor at the left-most position on the line.

To position the cursor at row r and column c, we use the statement

```
LOCATE r,c
```

We could use a loop to generate the spaces. However, there is an easier way. The string SPACE$(n) is a string of n spaces. By printing this string, we may "blank out" n spaces beginning at the current cursor position. Here is our subroutine:

```
5000 'Blank out line L
5010 LOCATE L,1:   'Position cursor at left of line L
5020 PRINT SPACE$(80)
5030 LOCATE L,1
5040 RETURN
```

Whenever we wish to use this subroutine, we first set the value of L to the line number to be erased. Next, we execute GOSUB 5000. Note that the value of L must be set before the GOSUB 5000 instruction is issued.

TEST YOUR UNDERSTANDING 2 (answer on page 131)

Write a subroutine that erases the first M columns of line L and positions the cursor in the upper left corner of the screen.

Example 2. Write a program that turns the computer into an electronic cash register. The program should accept as entries both taxable and nontaxable amounts. It should keep track of the totals of each. On command, it should display the totals, compute the tax, and compute the grand total owed.

Solution. A listing of the program is included below. This program illustrates some of the tricks involved in planning "user-friendly" programs. We allow the user to choose from four requests displayed on the screen. Such a display is called a **menu**. Here are the four possible requests.

1. **New Customer**. Zero all totals, clear the screen and display identifying headings as in Figure 5-2.

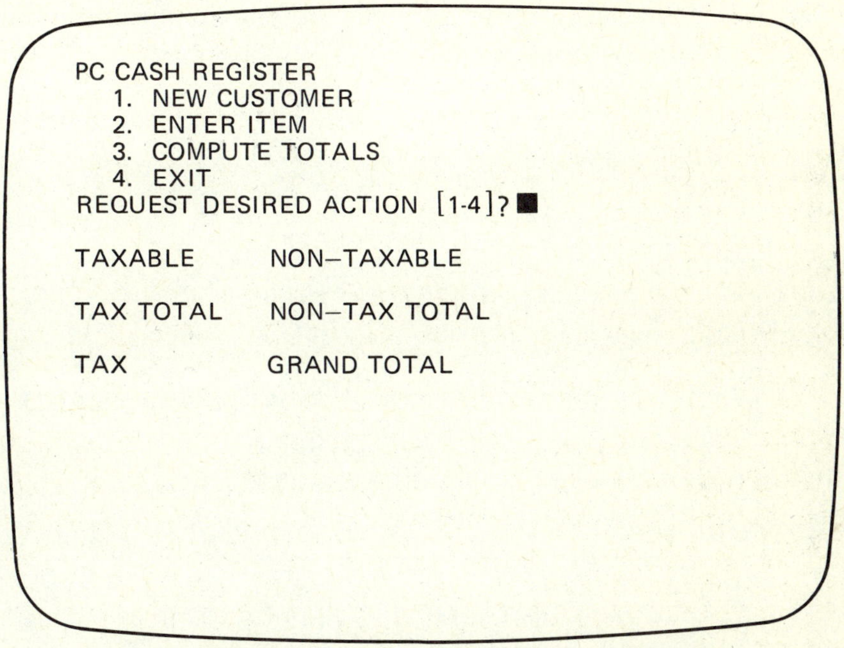

```
PC CASH REGISTER
   1. NEW CUSTOMER
   2. ENTER ITEM
   3. COMPUTE TOTALS
   4. EXIT
REQUEST DESIRED ACTION [1-4]? ■

TAXABLE       NON–TAXABLE

TAX TOTAL     NON–TAX TOTAL

TAX           GRAND TOTAL
```

Figure 5-2. Screen layout for the PC cash register.

2. **Enter item**. Accept the amount of an item. The program asks whether the item is taxable. The amount is displayed under the appropriate heading and is added to the appropriate total (taxable or non-taxable).
3. **Compute totals**. Compute tax and display totals.
4. **Exit**. End program.

The instructions for displaying the menu are in lines 1000-1080. Note that the subroutine to blank out a particular line begins in line 6000. In many parts of the program, we will want to write on a line. We will use the subroutine beginning in line 6000 to erase that particular line.

In line 1100 the user is asked to make a choice of activity from the menu by typing one of the numbers 1-4. Based on the user response,

128   Controlling the Flow of Your Program

the program goes to the subroutine at 2000, 3000, or 4000, or, in the case of choice 4, goes to line 5000 (no subroutine—More about that below). After the subroutine is executed, the program returns to the line after the one calling the subroutine and makes its way to line 1150. This line sends the program back to 1090, which erases line 7 and requests another activity. You may use the program all day. You may end the program by choosing option 4 on the menu.

Option 4 on the menu causes the program to go to line 5000, where the screen is cleared and the program is terminated. We did not use a subroutine to get to line 5000 since we did not expect to return. In this particular case, a GOSUB 5000 could have been used with no harm. Since the program ends, the computer will not look for a place to return. However, it is good programming practice to use a subroutine only in instances where the program is guaranteed to reach a RETURN instruction.

```
1000 'Display Menu
1010    CLS
1020    LOCATE 1,1:     'Home cursor
1030    PRINT "PC CASH REGISTER"
1040    PRINT "    1. NEW CUSTOMER"
1050    PRINT "    2. ENTER ITEM"
1060    PRINT "    3. COMPUTE TOTALS"
1070    PRINT "    4. EXIT"
1080    PRINT
1090    L=7:GOSUB 6000:     'Blank out entry line
1100    INPUT "REQUEST DESIRED ACTION (1-4)";REPLY$
1110    IF REPLY$="1" THEN GOSUB 2000
1120    IF REPLY$="2" THEN GOSUB 3000
1130    IF REPLY$="3" THEN GOSUB 4000
1140    IF REPLY$="4" THEN 5000
1150    GOTO 1090
2000 'New customer subroutine
2010    'Reset totals
2020    TAXABLE=0:NON-TAXABLE=0:GRANDTOTAL=0
2030    'Blank out lines 8-24 of screen
2040    FOR L=8 TO 20
2050       LOCATE L,1
2060       PRINT SPACE$(40)
2070    NEXT L
2080    'Print titles
2090    LOCATE 9,1
2100    PRINT "TAXABLE","NON-TAXABLE"
2110    LOCATE 12,1
2120    PRINT "TAX TOTAL","NON-TAX TOTAL"
2130    LOCATE 15,1
2140    PRINT "TAX", "GRAND TOTAL"
2150 RETURN
3000 'Enter item subroutine
3010    L=7:GOSUB 6000:     'Clear entry line
3020    INPUT "AMOUNT (NO DOLLAR SIGN)"; AMOUNT
3030    L=7:GOSUB 6000
3040    INPUT "TAXABLE=1,NON-TAXABLE=0";STATUS
3050    L=10:GOSUB 6000
```

```
3060    IF STATUS=1 THEN PRINT AMOUNT,""
3070    IF STATUS=0 THEN PRINT "",AMOUNT
3080    IF STATUS=1 THEN TAXABLE=TAXABLE+AMOUNT
3090    IF STATUS=0 THEN NONTAXABLE=NONTAXABLE+AMOUNT
3100 RETURN
4000 'Compute totals subroutine
4010    L=10:GOSUB 6000:      'Clear entry line
4020    L=13:GOSUB 6000:      'Clear first total line
4030    PRINT TAXABLE,NONTAXABLE
4040    TAX=.05*TAXABLE
4050    GRANDTOTAL=TAXABLE+TAX+NONTAXABLE
4060    L=16:GOSUB 6000
4070    PRINT TAX,GRANDTOTAL
4080 RETURN
5000 'Exit subroutine
5010 CLS
5020 END
6000 'Clear entry line L
6010    LOCATE L,1
6020    PRINT SPACE$(40):     'Clear Entry Line
6030    LOCATE L,1
6040 RETURN
```

> **TEST YOU UNDERSTANDING 3 (answer on page 131)**
>
> Enhance the program of Example 2 so that as a part of computing the totals, it asks you the amount presented ($10 bill, $20 bill, and so forth) and computes the change.

Nested Subroutines

In Example 2 we used a number of subroutines that were contained within subroutines. For example, lines 4000-4080 are a subroutine. However, on lines 4020 and 4030 we called the subroutine at 6000. Such subroutines are said to be **nested**. BASIC is able to handle such nesting. You may use nesting to any level. (A subroutine within a subroutine within a subroutine, and so forth.) However, you should be aware that a RETURN instruction always refers to the **innermost** subroutine. To put it another way, a RETURN always refers to the subroutine that was called most recently.

Caution: It is possible to accidentally create an infinite nesting of subroutines by repeatedly issuing GOSUB instructions, as in this program:

```
10 GOTO 20
20 GOSUB 10
```

The computer will eventually run out of memory to keep track of this nesting and an error will result.

Controlling the Flow of Your Program

The ON . . . GOSUB Instruction

In Example 2 we organized the program around four main subroutines, corresponding to the four possible choices on the MENU. It took several instructions to properly channel the program to the proper subroutine. BASIC provides a convenient shortcut for use in such situations: the ON. . .GOSUB instruction. The form of this instruction is:

```
ON <expression> GOSUB <line1>,<line2>,. . .
```

When BASIC encounters this instruction, it evaluates <expression>, which should yield an integer value; if the resulting value is 1, the program executes a GOSUB to <line1>; if the value is 2, the program executes a GOSUB to <line2>, and so forth. If the value is zero or more than the number of line numbers provided, the instruction will be ignored. (If <expression> yields a negative value, or an integer value larger than 255, an Illegal Function Call error results.)

For example, lines 1110-1130 of Example 2 may be replaced by the single line:

```
1110 ON VAL(REPLY$) GOSUB 2000,3000,4000
```

Here, the expression VAL(REPLY$) converts the string REPLY$ into its numerical equivalent ("1" converts to 1, "2" to 2, and so forth) . If this value is 1, the program executes a GOSUB 2000, if the value is 2, a GOSUB 3000 and if the value is 3, a GOSUB 4000.

Exercises (answers on page 370)

1. Write a subroutine that prints 10 asterisks (*) beginning at the left-most column of row L.
2. Write a subroutine that prints M asterisks beginning at the left-most column of row L.
3. Write a subroutine that prints M asterisks beginning at column K of row L.
4. Write a program that utilizes the subroutine of Exercise 3 to print rows of asterisks corresponding to K=5, L=3, M=30; K=4, L=5, M=35, K=8, L=7, and M=12
5. Consider this instruction:
    ```
    10 ON J=2 GOSUB 100,200,300,400,500
    ```
    What will be its effect if:

    (a) J=4 (b) J=7 (c) J=2 (d) J=10 (e) J=0 ?
6. Consider the program
    ```
    10 Y=5
    20 J=3
    30 S=Y-J
    40 ON S GOSUB 100,200,300,400
    ```

```
50 CLS
60 END
100 RETURN
200 RETURN
300 RETURN
400 RETURN
```

What are the two lines executed immediately after line 40?

ANSWERS TO TEST YOUR UNDERSTANDINGS 1, 2, and 3

1: 10-40-50-20-30

2:
```
5000 'Blank out 1st M columns of line L
5010 LOCATE L,1: 'Position cursor at left of line L
5020 PRINT SPACE$(M)
5030 LOCATE 1,1
5040 RETURN
```

3: Add the following program lines:
```
4071 LOCATE 20,1
4072 INPUT "AMOUNT PAID";PAID
4073 PRINT "PAID","CHANGE"
4074 PRINT PAID,PAID-GRANDTOTAL
```

Working With Data

6

6.1 Working With Tabular Data—Arrays

In Chapter 4 we introduced the notion of a variable and used variable names like:

AA, B1, CZ, W0

Unfortunately, the supply of variables available to us is not sufficient for many programs. Indeed, as we shall see in this chapter, there are relatively innocent programs which require hundreds or even thousands of variables. To meet the needs of such programs, BASIC allows for the use of so-called **subscripted variables**. Such variables are used constantly by mathematicians and are identified by numbered subscripts attached to a letter. For instance, here is a list of 1000 variables as they might appear in a mathematical work:

$A_1, A_2, A_3, \ldots, A_{1000}$

The numbers used to distinguish the variables are called **subscripts**. Likewise, the BASIC language allows definition of variables to be distinguished by subscripts. However, since the computer has difficulty placing the numbers in the traditional position, they are placed in parentheses on the same line as the letter. For example, the above list of 1000 different variables would be written in BASIC as

```
A(1),A(2),A(3),. . .,A(1000)
```

Please note that the variable A(1) is not the same as the variable A1. You may use both of them in the same program and BASIC will interpret them as being different.

A subscripted variable is really a group of variables with a common letter identification distinguished by different integer "subscripts." For instance, the above group of variables would constitute the subscripted variable A( ). It is often useful to view a subscripted variable as a table or array. For example, the subscripted variable A( ) considered above can be viewed as providing the following table of information:

A(1)
A(2)
A(3)
.
.
.
A(1000)

As shown here, the subscripted variable defines a table consisting of 1000 rows. Suppose that J is an integer between 1 and 1000. Then row number J contains a single entry, namely, the value of the variable A(J): The first row contains the value of A(1), the second the value of A(2), and so forth. Since a subscripted variable can be thought of as a table (or array), subscripted variables are often called **arrays**.

6.1 Working With Tabular Data—Arrays

The array shown above is a table consisting of 1000 rows and a single column. The IBM Personal Computer allows you to consider more general arrays. For example, consider the following financial table which records the daily income for three days from each of a chain of four computer stores:

	Store #1	Store #2	Store #3	Store #4
Jan.	1258.38	2437.46	4831.90	987.12
Feb.	1107.83	2045.68	3671.86	1129.47
March	1298.00	2136.88	4016.73	1206.34

This table has three rows and four columns. The entries may be stored in the computer as a set of 12 variables:

A(1,1)   A(1,2)   A(1,3)   A(1,4)
A(2,1)   A(2,2)   A(2,3)   A(2,4)
A(3,1)   A(3,2)   A(3,3)   A(3,4)

This array of variables is very similar to a subscripted variable except that there are now two subscripts. The first subscript indicates the row number and the second subscript indicates the column number. For example, the variable A(3,2) is in the third row, second column. A collection of variables such as that given above is called a **two-dimensional array** or a **doubly-subscripted variable**. Each setting of the variables in such an array defines a tabular array. For example, if we assign the values

A(1,1) = 1258.38, A(1,2) = 2437.46,
A(1,3) = 4831.90, and so forth,

then we will have the table of earnings from the computer store chain.

So far, we have only considered numeric arrays—arrays whose variables can assume only numerical values. However, it is possible to have arrays with variables that assume string values. (Recall that a string is a sequence of characters: letter, numeral, punctuation mark, or other printable keyboard symbol.) For example, here is an array which can contain string data:

A$(1)
A$(2)
A$(3)
A$(4)

Here the dollar signs indicate that each of the variables of the array is a string variable. If we assign the values

A$(1) = "SLOW", A$(2) = "FAST", A$(3) = "FAST", A$(4) = "STOP"

then the array is this table of words:

SLOW
FAST
FAST
STOP

Similarly, the employee record table

Social Security Number	Age	Sex	Marital Status
178654775	38	M	S
345861023	29	F	M
789257958	34	F	D
375486595	42	M	M
457696064	21	F	S

may be stored in an array of the form B$(I,J), where I assumes any one of the values 1, 2, 3, 4, 5 (I is the row), and J assumes any one of the values 1, 2, 3, 4 (J is the column). For example, B$(1,1) has the value "178654775", B$(1,2) has the value "38", B$(1,3) has the value "M", and so forth.

The IBM Personal Computer even allows you to have arrays which have three, four, or even more subscripts. For example, consider the computer store chain array introduced above. Suppose that we had one such array for each of ten consecutive years. This collection of data could be stored in a three-dimensional array of the form C(I,J,K), where I and J represent the row and column, just as before, and K represents the year. (K could assume the values 1,2,3,. . .,10.)

An array may involve any number of dimensions up to 255. The subscripts corresponding to each dimension may assume values from 0 to 32767. For all practical applications, any size array is permissible.

You must inform the computer of the sizes of the arrays you plan to use in a program. This allows the computer to allocate memory space to house all the values. To specify the size of an array, use a dimension (**DIM**) statement. For example, to define the size of the subscripted variable A(J), J=1,. . .,1000, we insert the statement

```
10 DIM A(1000)
```

in the program. This statement informs the computer to expect variables A(0), A(1), . . ., A(1000) in the program and that it should set aside memory space for 1001 variables. Note that in the absence of further instructions from you, BASIC begins all subscripts at 0. If you wish to use A(0), fine. If not, ignore it.

You need not use all the variables defined by a **DIM** statement. For example, in the case of the **DIM** statement above, you might actually use only the variables A(1), . . ., A(900). Don't worry about it! Just make sure that you have defined enough variables. Otherwise you could be in trouble. For example, in the case of the subscripted variable above, your program might make use of the variable A(1001). This will create an error condition. Suppose that this variable is used first in line 570. When you attempt to run the program, the computer will report

```
Subscript out of range in 570
```

Moreover, execution of the program will be halted. To fix the error merely redo the **DIM** statement to accommodate the undefined subscript.

6.1 Working With Tabular Data—Arrays 137

To define the size of a two-dimensional array, use a **DIM** statement of the form

```
10 DIM A(5,4)
```

This statement defines an array A(I,J) where I can assume the values 0, 1, 2, 3, 4, 5 and J can assume the values 0, 1, 2, 3, 4. Arrays with three or more subscripts are defined similarly.

TEST YOUR UNDERSTANDING 1 (answers on page 141)

Here is an array.

```
 12   645.80
148   489.75
589    12.89
487    14.50
```

a. Define an appropriate subscripted variable to store this data.
b. Define an appropriate **DIM** statement.

It is possible to dimension several arrays with one **DIM** statement. For example, the dimension statement

```
10 DIM A(1000), B$(5), A(5,4)
```

defines the array A(0), . . ., A(1000), the string array B$(0), . . ., B$(5) and the two-dimensional array A(I,J), I = 0, . . ., 5; J = 0, . . ., 4.

We now know how to set aside memory space for the variables of an array. We must next take up the problem of assigning values to these variables. We could use individual **LET** statements, but with 1000 variables in an array, this could lead to an unmanageable number of statements. There are more convenient methods that make use of loops. The next two examples illustrate two of these methods.

Example 1. Define an array A(J), J = 1, 2, . . ., 1000 and assign the following values to the variables of the array:

A(1) = 2, A(2) = 4, A(3) = 6, A(4) = 8, . . .

Solution. We wish to assign each variable a value equal to twice its subscript. That is, we wish to assign A(J) the value 2*J. To do this we use a loop:

```
10 DIM A(1000)
20 FOR J=1 TO 1000
30    A(J)=2*J
40 NEXT J
50 END
```

Note that the program ignores the variable A(0). Like any variable that has not been assigned a value, it has the value zero.

> **TEST YOUR UNDERSTANDING 2 (answer on page 141)**
>
> Write a program that assigns the variables A(0), ..., A(30) the values A(0) = 0, A(1) = 1, A(2) = 4, A(3) = 9, ...

When the computer is first turned on or reset, all variables (including those in arrays) are cleared. All numeric variables are set equal to 0, and all string variables are set equal to the null string (the string with no characters in it). If you wish to return all variables to this state during the execution of a program, use the **CLEAR** command. For example, when the computer encounters the command

```
570 CLEAR
```

it will reset all the variables. The **CLEAR** command can be convenient if, for example, you wish to use the same array to store two different sets of information at two different stages of the program. After the first use of the array you could then prepare for the second use by executing a **CLEAR**.

Example 2. Define an array corresponding to the employee record table above (page 136). Input the values given and print the table on the screen.

Solution. Our program will print the headings of the columns and then ask for the table entries, one row at a time. We will store the entries in the array B$(I,J), where I is one of 1, 2, 3, 4, or 5 and J is one of 1, 2, 3, or 4. We dimension the array as B$(5,4).

```
10 DIM B$(5,4)
20 FOR I=1 TO 5
30   INPUT "SS #,Age,Sex,Mar.St.";
        B$(I,1),B$(I,2),B$(I,3),B$(I,4)
40 NEXT I
50 CLS
60 PRINT "Soc. Sec. #", "Age", "Sex","Marital Status"
70 FOR I=1 TO 5
80   PRINT B$(I,1),B$(I,2),B$(I,3),B$(I,4)
90 NEXT I
100 END
```

Note that line 30 is a single program line, not two. It was typed without using the ENTER key until the end of the second physical line.

> **TEST YOUR UNDERSTANDING 3 (answer on page 141)**
>
> Suppose that your program uses a 9×2 array A$(I,J), a 9×1 array B$(I,J), and a 9×5 array C(I,J). Write an appropriate DIM statement(s).

If you plan to dimension an array, you should always insert the **DIM** statement before the variable first appears in your program. Otherwise, the first time BASIC comes across the array, it will assume that the subscripts go from 0 to 10. If it subsequently comes across a **DIM** statement, it will think you are changing the size of the array in the midst of the program, something which is not allowed. If you try to change the size of an array in the middle of a program, you will get this error message:

```
Duplicate Definition
```

In our discussion above, we have been very casual about ignoring unused subscripts, such as A(0). In some programs, there may be so many large arrays that memory space becomes precious. Sometimes, considerable memory space may be conserved by carefully planning which subscripts will be used and defining only those variables. You may eliminate unused 0 subscripts using the **OPTION BASE** statement. For example, the statement

```
10 OPTION BASE 1
```

begins all arrays with subscript 1. This statement must be used in a program prior to the dimensioning of any arrays.

Deleting Arrays

It is very simple to create an array that occupies a horrendous amount of memory space. For example, consider this seemingly harmless statement:

```
10 DIM A(10,10,10,10)
```

It defines an array with 10,000 entries. BASIC requires four bytes for each entry, so the array takes up 40,000 bytes of RAM! For this reason, you must do some planning so that your arrays do not overflow available memory. One technique for this involves deleting arrays from memory in order to make room for other arrays. You may do this using the **ERASE** statement. For example, to delete the above array we could use the statement

```
20 ERASE A
```

Once you execute ERASE, all the values of array A are lost and the DIM statement dimensioning A is canceled. In particular, you may redimension an array after an ERASE statement.

The **ERASE** statement may be used to delete several arrays at once, as in this statement:

```
30 ERASE B,C,D
```

Working With Data

Exercises (answers on page 371)

For each of the following tables, define an appropriate array and determine the appropriate **DIM** statement.

1. 5
   2
   1.7
   4.9
   11

2. 1.1 2.0 3.5
   1.7 2.4 6.2

3. JOHN
   MARY
   SIDNEY

4. 1 2 3

5. RENT   575.00
   UTILITIES   249.78
   CLOTHES   174.98
   CAR   348.70

6. Display the following array on the screen:

	Store #1	Receipts Store #2	Store #3
1/1-1/10	57,385.48	89,485.45	38,456.90
1/11-1/20	39,485.98	76,485.49	40,387.86
1/21-1/31	45,467.21	71,494.25	37,983.38

7. Write a program that displays the array of Exercise 6 along with totals of the receipts from each store.
8. Expand the program in Exercise 7 so that it calculates and displays the totals of ten-day periods. (Your screen will not be wide enough to display the ten-day totals in a fifth column, so display them in a separate array.)
9. Devise a program that keeps track of the inventory of an appliance store chain. Store the current inventory in an array of the form

	Store #1	Store #2	Store #3	Store #4
Refrig.				
Stove				
Air Cond.				
Vacuum				
Disposal				

   Your program should: (1) input the inventory corresponding to the beginning of the day, (2) continually ask for the next transaction—the store number and the number of appliances of each item sold, and (3) in response to each transaction, update the inventory array and redisplay it on the screen.

> **ANSWERS TO TEST YOUR UNDERSTANDINGS 1, 2, and 3**
>
> ```
> 1: a. A(I,J), I=1,2,3,4; J=1,2
>    b. DIM A(4,2)
> 2: 10 DIM A(30)
>    20 FOR J=0 TO 30
>    30    A(J)=J↑2
>    40 NEXT J
>    50 END
> 3: DIM A$(9,2),B$(9,1),C(9,5)
> ```

6.2 Inputting Data

In the preceding section we introduced arrays and discussed several methods for assigning values to the variables of an array. The most flexible method was via the **INPUT** statement. However, this can be a tedious method for large arrays. Fortunately, BASIC provides us with an alternate method for inputting data.

A given program may need many different numbers and strings. You may store the data needed in one or more **DATA** statements. A typical data statement has the form

```
10 DATA 3.457, 2.588, 11234, "WINGSPAN"
```

Note that this data statement consists of four data items, three numeric and one string. The data items are separated by commas. You may include as many data items in a single **DATA** statement as the line allows. Moreover, you may include any number of **DATA** statements in a program and they may be placed anywhere in the program, although a common placement is at the end of the program (just before the **END** statement). Note that we enclosed the string constant "WINGSPAN" in quotation marks. Actually this is not necessary. A string constant in a **DATA** statement does not need quotes, as long as it does not contain a comma, a colon, or start with a blank.

The **DATA** statements may be used to assign values to variables and, in particular, to variables in arrays. Here's how to do this. In conjunction with the **DATA** statements, you use one or more **READ** statements. For example, suppose that the above **DATA** statement appeared in a program. Further, suppose that you wish to assign these values:

```
A=3.457, B=2.588, C=11234, Z$="WINGSPAN"
```

This can be accomplished via the **READ** statement as shown here:

```
100 READ A,B,C,Z$
```

Here is how the **READ** statement works. On encountering a **READ** statement, the computer will look for a **DATA** statement. It will then assign values to the variables in the **READ** statement by taking the values, in order, from the **DATA** statement. If there is insufficient data in the first **DATA** statement, the computer will continue to assign values using the data in the next **DATA** statement. If necessary, the computer will proceed to the third **DATA** statement and so forth.

TEST YOUR UNDERSTANDING 1 (answer on page 147)

Assign the following values:
A(1)=5.1, A(2)=4.7, A(3)=5.8, A(4)=3.2, A(5)=7.9, A(6)=6.9.

The computer maintains an internal pointer which points to the next **DATA** item to be used. If the computer encounters a second **READ** statement, it will start reading where it left off. For example, suppose that instead of the above **READ** statement, we use the two read statements

```
100 READ A,B
200 READ C,Z$
```

Upon encountering the first statement, the computer will look for the location of the pointer. Initially, it will point to the first item in the first **DATA** statement. The computer will assign the values A=3.457 and B=2.588. Moreover, the position of the pointer will be advanced to the third item in the **DATA** statement. Upon encountering the next **READ** statement, the computer will assign values beginning with the one designated by the pointer, namely C=11234 and Z$="WINGSPAN".

TEST YOUR UNDERSTANDING 2 (answer on page 147)

What values are assigned to A and B$ by the following program?

```
10 DATA 10,30,"ENGINE","TACH"
20 READ A,B
30 READ C$,B$
40 END
```

The following example illustrates the use of **DATA** statements in assigning values to an array.

Example 1. Suppose that the monthly electricity costs of a certain family are as follows:

Jan.	$89.74	Feb.	$95.84	March	$79.42
Apr.	78.93	May	72.11	June	115.94
July	158.92	Aug.	164.38	Sep.	105.98
Oct.	90.44	Nov.	89.15	Dec.	93.97

Write a program calculating the average monthly cost of electricity.

Solution. Let us unceremoniously dump all of the numbers shown above into **DATA** statements at the end of the program. Arbitrarily, let's start the **DATA** statements at line 1000, with **END** at 2000. This allows us plenty of room. To calculate the average, we must add up the numbers and divide by 12. To do this, let us first create an array A(J), J = 1, 2, . . ., 12 and set A(J) equal to the cost of electricity in the Jth month. We do this via a loop and the **READ** statement. We then use a loop to add all the A(J)'s. Finally, we divide by 12 and PRINT the answer. Here is the program.

```
10 DIM A(12)
20 FOR J=1 TO 12
30   READ A(J)
40 NEXT J
50 C=0
60 FOR J=1 TO 12
70   C=C+A(J):      'C ACCUMULATES THE SUM OF THE A(J)
80 NEXT J
90 C=C/12 :          'DIVIDE SUM BY 12
100 PRINT "THE AVERAGE MONTHLY COST OF ELECTRICITY
     IS",C
1000 DATA 89.74, 95.84, 79.42, 78.93, 72.11, 115.94
1010 DATA 158.92, 164.38, 105.98, 90.44, 89.15, 93.97
2000 END
```

The following program could be helpful in preparing the payroll of a small business.

Example 2. A small business has five employees. Here are their names and hourly wages.

Name	Hourly Wage
Joe Polanski	7.75
Susan Greer	8.50
Allan Cole	8.50
Betsy Palm	6.00
Herman Axler	6.00

Write a program which accepts as input hours worked for the current week and which calculates the current gross pay and the amount of Social Security tax to be withheld from their pay. (Assume that the Social Security tax amounts to 6.70 percent of gross pay.)

Solution. Let us keep the hourly wage rates and names in two arrays, called A(J) and B$(J), respectively, where J = 1, 2, 3, 4, and 5. Note that we can't use a single two-dimensional array for this data since the names are string data and the hourly wage rates are numerical. (Recall that BASIC does not let us mix the two kinds of data in an array.) The first part of the program will be to assign the values to the variables in the two arrays. Next, the program will, one by one, print out the names of the employees and ask for the number of hours worked during the current week. This data will be stored in the array C(J), J = 1, 2, 3, 4, 5. The program will then compute the gross wages as A(J)*C(J) (that is, <wage rate> times <number of hours worked>). This piece of data will be stored in the array D(J), J = 1, 2, 3, 4, 5. Next, the program will compute the amount of Social Security tax to be withheld as .0670*D(J). This piece of data will be stored in the array E(J), J = 1, 2, 3, 4, 5. Finally, all the computed data will be printed on the screen. Here is the program:

```
10 DIM A(5),B$(5),C(5),D(5),E(5)
20 FOR J=1 TO 5
30   READ B$(J),A(J)
40 NEXT J
50 FOR J=1 TO 5
60   PRINT "TYPE CURRENT HOURS OF", B$(J)
70   INPUT C(J)
80   D(J)=A(J)*C(J)
90   E(J)=.0670*D(J)
100 NEXT J
110 PRINT "EMPLOYEE","GROSS WAGES","SOC.SEC.TAX"
120 FOR J=1 TO 5
130   PRINT B$(J),D(J),E(J)
140 NEXT J
200 DATA JOE POLANSKI, 7.75, SUSAN GREER, 8.50
210 DATA ALLAN COLE, 8.50, BETSY PALM, 6.00
220 DATA HERMAN AXLER, 6.00
1000 END
```

In certain applications you may wish to read the same **DATA** statements more than once. To do this you must reset the pointer via the **RESTORE** statement. For example, consider the following program.

```
10 DATA 2.3, 5.7, 4.5, 7.3
20 READ A,B
30 RESTORE
40 READ C,D
50 END
```

Line 20 sets A equal to 2.3 and B equal to 5.7. The **RESTORE** statement of line 30 moves the pointer back to the first item of data, 2.3. The **READ** statement of line 40 then sets C equal to 2.3 and D equal to 5.7. Note that without the **RESTORE** in line 30, the **READ** statement in line 40 would set C equal to 4.5 and D equal to 7.3.

There are two common errors in using **READ** and **DATA** statements. First, you may instruct the program to **READ** more data than is present in the **DATA** statements. For example, consider the following program.

```
10 DATA 1,2,3,4
20 FOR J=1 TO 5
30    READ A(J)
40 NEXT J
50 END
```

This program attempts to read five pieces of data, but the **DATA** statement only has four. In this case, you will receive an error message:

```
Out of data in 30
```

A second common error is attempting to assign a string value to a numeric variable or vice versa. Such an attempt will lead to a **Type mismatch** error.

6.2 Inputting Data

Exercises (answers on page 372)

Each of the following programs assigns values to the variables of an array. Determine which values are assigned.

1.
```
10 DIM A(10)
20 FOR J=1 TO 10
30    READ A(J)
40 NEXT J
50 DATA 2,4,6,8,10,12,14,16,18,20
100 END
```
2.
```
10 DIM A(3),B(3)
20 FOR J=0 TO 3
30    READ A(J), B(J)
40 NEXT J
50 DATA 1.1,2.2,3.3,4.4,5.5,6.6,7.7,8.8,9.9
60 END
```
3.
```
10 DIM A(3),B$(3)
20 FOR J=0 TO 3
30    READ A(J)
40 NEXT J
50 FOR J=0 TO 3
60    READ B$(J)
70 NEXT J
80 DATA 1,2,3,4,A,B,C,D
90 END
```
4.
```
10 DIM A(3), B(3)
20 READ A(0),B(0)
30 READ A(1),B(1)
40 RESTORE
50 READ A(2),B(2)
60 READ A(3),B(3)
70 DATA 1,2,3,4,5,6,7,8
80 END
```
5.
```
10 DIM A(3,4)
20 FOR I=1 TO 3
30    FOR J=1 TO 4
40       READ A(I,J)
50    NEXT J
60 NEXT I
70 DATA 1,2,3,4,5,6,7,8,9,10,11,12
80 END
```
6.
```
10 DIM A(3,4)
20 FOR J=1 TO 4
30    FOR I=1 TO 3
40       READ A(I,J)
50    NEXT I
60 NEXT J
```

```
70 DATA 1,2,3,4,5,6,7,8,9,10,11,12
80 END
```

Each of the following programs contains an error. Find it.

7.
```
10 DIM A(5)
20 FOR J=1 TO 5
30    READ A(J)
40 NEXT J
50 DATA 1,2,3,4
60 END
```

8.
```
10 DIM A(5)
20 FOR J=1 TO 5
30    READ A(J)
40 NEXT J
50 DATA 1,A,2,B
60 END
```

9. Here is a table of Federal Income Tax Withholding of weekly wages for an individual claiming one exemption. Assume that each of the employees, in the business discussed in the text, claims a single exemption. Modify the program given so that it correctly computes Federal Withholding and the net amount of wages. (That is, the total after Federal Withholding and Social Security are deducted.)

Wages at Least	But Less Than	Tax Withheld
200	210	29.10
210	220	31.20
220	230	33.80
230	240	36.40
240	250	39.00
250	260	41.60
260	270	44.20
270	280	46.80
280	290	49.40
290	300	52.10
300	310	55.10
310	320	58.10
320	330	61.10
330	340	64.10
340	350	67.10

10. Here is a set of 24 hourly temperature reports as compiled by the National Weather Service. Write a program to compute the average temperature for the last 24 hours. Let your program respond to a query concerning the temperature at a particular hour. (For example, what was the temperature at 2:00 PM?)

	AM	PM
12:00	10	38
1:00	10	39
2:00	9	40
3:00	9	40
4:00	8	42
5:00	11	38
6:00	15	33
7:00	18	27

6.2 Inputting Data   147

```
              AM      PM
    8:00      20      22
    9:00      25      18
   10:00      31      15
   11:00      35      12
```

ANSWERS TO TEST YOUR UNDERSTANDINGS 1 and 2

```
1: 10  DATA 5.1,4.7,5.8,3.2,7.9,6.9
   20  FOR J=1 TO 6
   30    READ A(J)
   40  NEXT J
   50  END
2: A = 10, B$ = "TACH"
```

6.3 Formatting Your Output

In this section we will discuss the various ways of formatting output on the screen and on the printer. IBM Personal Computer BASIC is quite flexible in the form in which you can cast output. You have control over the size of the letters on the screen, placement of output on the line, degree of accuracy to which calculations are displayed, and so forth. Let us begin by reviewing what we have already learned about printing.

Semicolons in PRINT Statements

The IBM Personal Computer screen may be set for 40- or 80-character lines, using the **WIDTH** statement. This gives 40 or 80 print positions in each line. These are divided into print zones of 14 characters each.* To start printing at the beginning of the next print zone, insert a comma between the items to be printed.

In many applications, it is necessary to print more columns than there are print zones. Or, output may look better if the columns are less than a full print zone wide. To avoid any space between consecutive print items, separate them in the PRINT statement by a semicolon. Consider the following instruction:

```
10 PRINT "PERSO";"NAL COMPUTER"
```

It will result in the output

```
PERSONAL COMPUTER
```

---

* For an 80-column width, the last print zone has only 10 characters. For a 40-column width, the last print zone has only 12 characters.

148 Working With Data

The semicolon suppresses any space between the display of PERSO and NAL COMPUTER.

In displaying numbers, remember that all positive numbers begin with a blank space, which is in place of the understood plus (+) sign. Negative numbers, however, have a displayed minus (−) sign and do not begin with a blank space. For example, the statement

```
20 PRINT "THE VALUE OF A IS";2.35
```

will result in the display

```
THE VALUE OF A IS 2.35
```

The space between the S and the 2 comes from the blank which is considered part of the number 2.35. On the other hand, the statement

```
30 PRINT "THE VALUE OF A IS";-2.35
```

will result in the display

```
THE VALUE OF A IS-2.35
```

To obtain a space between the S and the −, we must include a space in the string constant.

```
30 PRINT "THE VALUE OF A IS ";-2.35
```

TEST YOUR UNDERSTANDING 1 (answer on page 155)

Write a program that allows you to input two numbers. The program should then display them as an addition problem in the form 5+7=12.

At the completion of a PRINT statement, BASIC will automatically supply an ENTER so that the cursor moves to the beginning of the next line. You may suppress this ENTER by ending the PRINT statement with a semicolon. For example, the statements

```
40 PRINT "THE VALUE OF A IS";
50 PRINT 2.35
```

will result in the display

```
THE VALUE OF A IS 2.35
```

TEST YOUR UNDERSTANDING 2 (answer on page 155)

Describe the output from the following program:

```
10 A=5:B=3:C=8
20 PRINT "THE VALUE OF A IS",A
30 PRINT "THE VALUE OF B";
40 PRINT "IS";B
50 PRINT "THE VALUE OF C IS";-C
```

Our discussion above was oriented to the display of data on the screen. However, you may also use semicolons in LPRINT statements to control spacing of output on the printer.

Horizontal Tabbing

You may begin a print item in any print position. To do this use the **TAB** command. The print positions are numbered from 1 to 255, going from left to right. (Note that a line may be up to 255 characters long. On the screen an oversized line will wrap around to the next line. However, the line will print correctly on a printer having a wide enough print line.) The statement TAB(7) means to move to column 7. **TAB** is always used in conjunction with a **PRINT** statement. For example, the print statement

```
50 PRINT TAB(7) A
```

will print the value of the variable A beginning in print position 7. It is possible to use more than one **TAB** per **PRINT** statement. For example, the statement

```
100 PRINT TAB(5) A; TAB(15) B
```

will print the value of A beginning in print position 5 and the value of B beginning in print position 15. Note the semicolon between the two **TAB** instructions.

TEST YOUR UNDERSTANDING 3 (answer on page 155)

Write an instruction printing the value of A in column 25 and the value of B seven columns further to the right.

In some applications you may wish to to add a certain number of spaces between output items (as opposed to TABbing where the next item appears in a specified column). This may be accomplished using the SPC (space) function, which works very much like TAB. For example, to print the values of A and B with 5 blank spaces between them, we may use the statement

```
110 PRINT A; SPC(5) B
```

Formatting Numbers

IBM Personal Computer BASIC has rather extensive provisions for formatting numerical output. Here are some of the things you may specify with regard to printing a number:

- Number of digits of accuracy
- Alignment of columns (one's column, ten's column, hundred's column, and so forth)

150 Working With Data

- Display and positioning of the initial dollar sign
- Display of commas in large numbers (as in 1,000,000)
- Display and positioning of + and − signs.

All of these formatting options may be requested with the **PRINT USING** statement. Roughly speaking, you tell the computer what you wish your number to look like by specifying a "prototype." For example, suppose you wish to print the value of the variable A with four digits to the left of the decimal point and two digits to the right. This could be done via the instruction

```
10 PRINT USING "####.##"; A
```

Here, each # stands for a digit and the period stands for the decimal point. If, for example, A was equal to 5432.381, this instruction would round the value of A to the specified two decimal places and would print the value of A as

```
5432.38
```

On the other hand, if the value of A was 932.547, then the computer would print the value as

```
932.55
```

In this case, the value is printed with a leading blank space since the format specified four digits to the left of the decimal point. This sort of printing is especially useful in aligning columns of figures like this:

```
  367.1
 1567.2
29573.3
    2.4
```

The above list of numbers could be printed using the following program:

```
10 DATA 367.1, 1567.2, 29573.3, 2.4
20 FOR J=1 TO 4
30   READ A(J)
40   PRINT USING "#####.#";A(J)
50 NEXT J
60 END
```

TEST YOUR UNDERSTANDING 4 (answer on page 155)

Write an instruction which prints the number 456.75387 rounded to two decimal places.

You may use a single **PRINT USING** statement to print several numbers on the same line. For example, the statement

```
10 PRINT USING "##.##"; A,B,C
```

will print the values of A, B, and C on the same line, all in the format ##.##. Only one space will be allowed between each of the numbers.

Additional spaces may be added by using extra #'s. If you wish to print numbers on one line in two different formats, then you must use two different **PRINT USING** statements, with the first ending in a semicolon (;) to indicate a continuation on the same line.

If you try to display a number larger than the prototype, the number will be displayed preceded by a percent (%) symbol. For example, consider the statement

```
10 PRINT USING "###"; A
```

If the value of A is 5000, then the display will look like

```
%5000
```

> **TEST YOUR UNDERSTANDING 5 (answer on page 155)**
>
> Write a program to calculate and display the numbers 2^J, $J = 1, 2, 3, \ldots, 15$. The columns of the numbers should be properly aligned on the right.

You may have the computer insert a dollar sign on a displayed number. The following two statements illustrate the procedure:

```
10 PRINT USING "$####.##"; A
20 PRINT USING "$$####.##";A
```

Suppose that the value of A is 34.78. The results of lines 10 and 20 will then be displayed:

```
$   34.78
$34.78
```

Note the difference between the displays produced by lines 10 and 20. The single $ produces a dollar sign in the fifth position to the left of the decimal point. This is just to the left of the four digits specified in the prototype ####.##. However, the $$ in line 20 indicates a "floating dollar sign." The dollar sign is printed in the first position to the left of the number without leaving any space.

Example 1. Here is a list of checks written by a family during the month of March.

$15.32, $387.00, $57.98, $3.47, $15.88

Print the list of checks on the screen with the columns properly aligned and the total displayed below the list of check amounts, in the form of an addition problem.

Solution. We first read the check amounts into an array A(J), J = 1, 2, 3, 4, 5. While we read the amounts, we accumulate the total in the variable B. We use a second loop to print the display in the desired format.

```
10 DATA 15.32, 387.00, 57.98, 3.47, 15.88
20 FOR J=1 TO 5
```

152   Working With Data

```
30   READ A(J)
40   B=B+A(J)
50   PRINT USING "$###.##"; A(J)
60 NEXT J
70 PRINT "_____"
80 PRINT USING "$###.##"; B
90 END
```

Here is what the output will look like:

```
$ 15.32
$387.00
$ 57.98
$  3.47
$ 15.88
―――――――
$479.65
```

Note that line 70 is used to print the line under the column of figures.

The **PRINT USING** statement has several other variations. To print commas in large numbers, insert a comma anywhere to the left of the decimal point. For example, consider the statement

```
10 PRINT USING ###,###; A
```

If the value of A is 123456, it will be displayed as:

```
123,456
```

The **PRINT USING** statement may also be used to position plus and minus signs in connection with displayed numbers. A plus sign at the beginning or the end of a prototype will cause the appropriate sign to the printed in the position indicated. For example, consider the statement

```
10 PRINT USING "+####.###"; A
```

Suppose that the value of A is −458.73. It will be displayed as

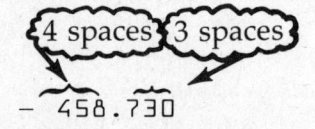

⎯⎯⎯ 4 spaces ⎯⎯⎯ 3 spaces

```
-   458.730
```

Similarly, consider the statement

```
10 PRINT USING "+###.##"; A
```

Suppose that A has the value .05873. Then A will be displayed as

⎯⎯⎯ 3 spaces ⎯⎯⎯ 2 spaces

```
+   .06
```

Important Note: In the above discussion, we have only mentioned output on the screen. However, all of the features mentioned may be used on a printer via the **LPRINT USING** instruction. Note, however, that the wider line of the printer allows you to display more data than the screen. In particular, there are more 14-character print fields (just how many depends on which printer you own), and you may **TAB** to a higher numbered column than on the screen.

Recall that BASIC uses two different representations for numbers–the usual decimal representation and scientific (or exponential notation). You may use ^^^^ to format numbers into scientific notation. For example, to display a number in scientific notation with two digits to the left of the decimal point and two to the right, you would use the format string

`"###.##^^^^"`

In this format, the number 100 would be displayed as

`10.00E+01`

Other Variants of PRINT USING

There are several further things you can do with the **PRINT USING** statement. They are especially useful to accountants and others concerned with preparing financial documents.

If you precede the prototype with **, this will cause all unused digit positions in a number to be filled with asterisks. For example, consider the statement

`10 PRINT USING "**####.#";A`

If A has the value 34.86, the value will be displayed as

`****34.9`

Note that four asterisks are displayed since six digits to the left of the decimal point are specified in the prototype (the asterisks count), but the value of A uses only two. The remaining four are filled with asterisks.

You may combine the action of ** and $. You should experiment with this combination. It is especially useful for printing dollar amounts of the form

`$*******387.98`

Such a format is especially useful in printing amounts on checks to prevent modification.

By using a minus sign (−) immediately after a prototype, you will print the appropriate number with a trailing minus sign if it is negative and with no sign if it is positive. For example, the statement

`10 PRINT USING "####.##-"; A`

with A equal to −57.88 will result in the display:

`57.88-`

On the other hand, if A is equal to 57.88, the display will be

`57.88`

This format for numbers is often used in preparing accounting reports.

154 Working With Data

Exercises (answer on page 373)

Write programs that generate the following displays. The lines of dots are not meant to be displayed. They are furnished for you to judge spacing.

1. THE VALUE OF X IS 5.378

2. THE VALUE OF X IS   5.378

3. DATE   QTY   @   COST   DISCOUNT   NET COST

4.
```
     6.753
    15.111
   111.850
     6.702
   ────────
```

5.
```
   $  12.82
   $117.58
   $   5.87
   $    .99
   $    .99
   ────────
```

   Calculate   Calculate
   Sum   Sum

6.
```
                            Date   3/18/81
   Pay to the Order of  Wildcatters, Inc.
   The sum of             *********$89,385.00
```

7.
```
     5,787
       387
   127,486
    38,531
   ────────
   Calculate
   Sum
```

8.
```
   $385.41
   - $17.85
   ────────
   Calculate
   Difference
```

9. Write a program that prints a number rounded to the nearest integer. For example, if the input is 11.7, the output is 12. If the input is 158.2, the output is 158. Your program should accept the number to be rounded via an INPUT statement.

10. Write a program that allows your computer to function as a cash register. Let the program accept purchase amounts via INPUT statements. Let the user tell the program when the list of INPUTs is complete. The program should then print out the purchase amounts, with dollar signs and columns aligned, compute the total purchase, add 5 percent sales tax, compute the total amount due, ask for the amount paid, and compute the change due.

11. Prepare the display of Exercise 4 using 40 characters per line.

> **ANSWERS TO TEST YOUR UNDERSTANDINGS 1, 2, 3, 4, and 5**
>
> 1: ```
>   10 INPUT A,B
>   20 PRINT A;"+";B;"=";A+B
>   30 END
>    ```
> 2: ```
>   THE VALUE OF A IS   5
>   THE VALUE OF B IS 3
>   THE VALUE OF C IS-8
>    ```
> 3: `10 PRINT TAB(25) A;TAB(32) B`
> 4: `10 PRINT USING "###.##"; 456.7587`
> 5: ```
>   10 FOR J=1 TO 15
>   20 PRINT USING "#####"; 2^J
>   30 NEXT J
>   40 END
>    ```

6.4 Gambling With Your Computer

One of the most interesting features of your computer is its ability to generate events whose outcomes are "random." For example, you may instruct the computer to "throw a pair of dice" and produce a random pair of integers between 1 and 6. You may instruct the computer to "pick a card at random from a deck of 52 cards." You may also program the computer to choose a two-digit number "at random". And so forth. The source of all such random choices is the BASIC function **RND**. To explain how this function works, let us consider the following program:

```
10 FOR X=1 TO 500
20    PRINT RND
30 NEXT X
40 END
```

This program consists of a loop which prints 500 numbers, each called **RND**. Each of these numbers lies between 0.000000 (inclusive) and 1.000000 (exclusive). Each time the program refers to **RND** (as in line 20 here), the computer makes a "random" choice from among the numbers in the indicated range. This is the number that is printed.

To obtain a better idea of what we are talking about, you should generate some random numbers using a program like the one above. Unless you have a printer, 500 numbers will be too many for you to look at in one viewing. You should print four random numbers on one line (one per print zone) and limit yourself to 25 displayed lines at one time. Here is a partial print-out of such a program.

```
.245121    .305003    .311866    .515163
.984546    .901159    .727313    6.83401E-03
.896609    .660212    .554489    .818675
.583931    .448163    .86774     .0331043
.137119    .226544    .215274    .876763
```

156 Working With Data

What makes these numbers "random" is that the procedure the computer uses to select them is "unbiased," with all numbers having an equal likelihood of selection. Moreover, if you generate a large collection of random numbers, then numbers between 0 and .1 will compose approximately 10 percent of those chosen, those between .5 and 1.0 will compose 50 percent of those chosen, and so forth. In some sense, the random number generator provides a uniform sample of the numbers between 0 and 1.

> **TEST YOUR UNDERSTANDING 1 (answer on page 163)**
>
> Assume that RND is used to generate 1000 numbers. Approximately how many of these numbers would you expect to lie between .6 and .9?

The random number generator is controlled by a so-called "seed" number, which controls the sequence of numbers generated. Once a particular seed number has been chosen, the sequence of random numbers is fixed. This would make computer games of chance rather boring since they would always generate the same sequence of play. This may be prevented by changing the seed number using the **RANDOMIZE** command. A command of the form

```
10 RANDOMIZE
```

will cause the computer to print out the display

```
Random Number Seed (-32768 to 32767)?
```

You then respond with a number in the indicated interval. Suppose, for example, you choose 129. The computer will then reseed the random number generator with the seed 129 and will generate the sequence of random numbers corresponding to this seed. Another method of choosing a seed number is with a command of this form:

```
20 RANDOMIZE 129
```

This command sets the seed number to 129 without asking you. In Chapter 13, we will show you how to use the computer's internal clock to provide a seed number. This is a method of generating a seed over which no one has any control.

The function **RND** generates random numbers lying between 0 and 1. However, in many applications, we will require randomly chosen **integers** lying in a certain range. For example, suppose that we wish to generate random integers chosen from among 1, 2, 3, 4, 5, and 6. Let us multiply **RND** by 6 to obtain **6*RND**. This is a random number between 0.00000 and 5.99999. Next, let us add 1 to this number. Then 6*RND+1 is a random number between 1.00000 and 6.99999. To obtain integers from among 1, 2, 3, 4, 5, and 6, we must "chop off" the decimal portion of the number 6*RND+1. To do this we use the INT function. If X is any number, then INT(X) is the largest integer less than or equal to X. For example,

INT(5.23)=5, INT(7.99)=7, INT(100.001)=100

Be careful in using INT with negative X. The definition we gave is correct, but unless you think things through, it is easy to make an error. For example,

INT(-7.4)=-8

since the largest integer less than or equal to -7.4 is equal to -8. (Draw -7.4 and -8 on a number line to see the point!) Let us get back to our random numbers. To chop off the decimal portion of 6*RND+1, we compute INT(6*RND+1). This last expression is a random number from among 1, 2, 3, 4, 5, 6. Similarly, the expression

INT(100*RND+1)

may be used to generate random numbers from among the integers 1, 2, 3,..., 100.

> **TEST YOUR UNDERSTANDING 2 (answer on page 163)**
>
> Generate random integers from 0 to 1. (This is the computer analogue of flipping a coin: 0=heads, 1=tails.) Run this program to generate 50 coin tosses. How many heads and how many tails occur?

Example 1. Write a program that turns the computer into a pair of dice. Your program should report the number rolled on each as well as the total.

Solution. We will hold the value of die #1 in the variable X and the value of die #2 in variable Y. The program will compute values for X and Y, print out the values and the total X+Y.

```
5    RANDOMIZE
10   CLS
20   X=INT(6*RND + 1)
30   Y=INT(6*RND + 1)
40   PRINT "LADIES AND GENTLEMEN, BETS PLEASE!"
50   INPUT "ARE ALL BETS DOWN(Y/N)"; A$
60   IF A$="Y" THEN 100 ELSE 40
100  PRINT "THE ROLL IS",X,Y
110  PRINT "THE WINNING TOTAL IS " ; X+Y
120  INPUT "PLAY AGAIN(Y/N)"; B$
130  IF B$="Y" THEN 10
200  PRINT "THE CASINO IS CLOSING. SORRY!"
210  END
```

Note the use of computer-generated conversation on the screen. Also note how the program uses lines 120-130 to allow the player to control how many times the game will be played. Finally, note the use of the command **RANDOMIZE** in line 5. This will generate a question to allow you to choose a seed number.

> **TEST YOUR UNDERSTANDING 3 (answer on page 163)**
> Write a program that flips a "biased coin." Let it report "heads" one-third of the time and tails two-thirds of the time.

You may enhance the realism of a gambling program by letting the computer keep track of bets as in the following example.

Example 2. Write a program that turns the computer into a roulette wheel. Let the computer keep track of bets and winnings for up to five players. For simplicity, assume that the only bets are on single numbers. (In the next example we will let you remove this restriction!)

Solution. A roulette wheel has 38 positions: 1-36, 0, and 00. In our program we will represent these as the numbers 1-38, with 37 corresponding to 0 and 38 corresponding to 00. A spin of the wheel will consist of choosing a random integer between 1 and 38. The program will start by asking for the number of players. For a typical spin of the wheel, the program will ask for bets by each player. A bet will consist of a number (1-38) and an amount bet. The wheel will then spin. The program will determine the winners and losers. A payoff for a win is 32 times the amount bet. Each player has an account, stored in an array A(J), J=1, 2, 3, 4, 5. At the end of each spin, the accounts are adjusted and displayed. Just as in Example 1, the program asks if another play is desired. Here is the program.

```
5     RANDOMIZE
10    INPUT "NUMBER OF PLAYERS";N
20    DIM A(5),B(5),C(5):     'At Most 5 Players
30    FOR J=1 TO N :          'Initial Purchase of Chips
40      PRINT "PLAYER "; J
50      INPUT "HOW MANY CHIPS"; A(J)
60    NEXT J
100   PRINT "LADIES AND GENTLEMEN! PLACE YOUR BETS
      PLEASE!"
110   FOR J=1 TO N :          'Place Bets
120     PRINT "PLAYER "; J
130     INPUT "NUMBER, AMOUNT"; B(J),C(J):'INPUT BET
140   NEXT J
200   X=INT(38*RND + 1):      'Spin the wheel
220   PRINT "THE WINNER IS NUMBER"; X
300   'Compute winnings and losses
310   FOR J=1 TO N
320     IF X=B(J) THEN 400
330     A(J)=A(J)-C(J):        'Player J loses
340     PRINT "PLAYER ";J;"LOSES"
350     GOTO 420
400     A(J)=A(J)+32*C(J):     'Player J wins
410     PRINT "PLAYER ";J;"WINS "; 32*C(J); "DOLLARS"
```

6.4 Gambling With Your Computer

```
420 NEXT J
430 PRINT "PLAYER BANKROLLS":      'Display game status
440 PRINT
450 PRINT "PLAYER", "CHIPS"
460 FOR J=1 TO N
470   PRINT J,A(J)
480 NEXT J
500 INPUT "DO YOU WISH TO PLAY ANOTHER ROLL(Y/N)";R$
510 CLS
520 IF R$="Y" THEN 100:     'Repeat game
530 PRINT "THE CASINO IS CLOSED. SORRY!"
600 END
```

You should try a few spins of the wheel. The program is fun as well as instructive. Note that the program allows you to bet more chips than you have. We will leave it to the exercises to add in a test that there are enough chips to cover the bet. You could also build lines of credit into the game! In the next example, we will illustrate how the roulette program may be extended to incorporate the bets EVEN and ODD.

Before we proceed to the next example, however, let's discuss one further defect of the program in Example 2. Note that line 5 contains a RANDOMIZE statement. The program will then ask for a random number seed. The person who selects the random number seed has control over the random number sequence and hence over the game. This is most unsatisfactory. However, there is a simple way around this difficulty.

The IBM PC has an internal clock which is set each time you sign on the computer. This clock keeps track of time in hours, minutes, and seconds. The value of the clock is accessed via the function **TIME$**. We will discuss use of the clock in detail in Chapter 13. For the moment, however, let's borrow a fact from that discussion. The current reading of the seconds portion of the clock is equal to:

```
VAL(RIGHT$(TIME$,2))
```

Let's use this number as our random number seed. (It is unlikely that anyone can control the precise second at which the game begins.)

Example 3. Modify the roulette program of Example 2, so that it allows bets on EVEN and ODD. A one-dollar bet on either of these pays one dollar in winnings.

Solution. Our program will now allow three different bets: on a number and on EVEN or ODD. Let us design subroutines, corresponding to each of these bets, which determine whether player J wins or loses. For each subroutine, let X be the number (1-38) that results from spinning the wheel. In the preceding program, a bet by player J was described by two numbers: B(J) equals the number bet and C(J) equals the amount bet. Now let us add a third number to describe a bet. Let D(J) equal 1 if J bets on a number, 2 if J bets on EVEN, and 3 if J bets on odd. In case D(J) is 2 or 3, we will again let C(J) equal the amount bet, but B(J) will be ignored. The subroutine for determining the winners of bets on numbers can be obtained by making small modifications to the corresponding portion of our previous program, as follows:

```
1000 'Bet=NUMBER
1010     IF B(J)=X THEN 1050
1020     PRINT "PLAYER ";J; " LOSES"
1030     A(J)=A(J)-C(J)
1040     GOTO 1070
1050     PRINT "PLAYER ";J; " WINS"; 32*C(J); "DOLLARS"
1060     A(J)=A(J) + 32*C(J)
1070 RETURN
```

Here is the subroutine corresponding to the bet EVEN.

```
2000 'Bet=EVEN
2010     K=0
2020     IF X=2*K THEN 2070 ELSE 2030
2030     K=K+1: IF K>=20 THEN 2040 ELSE 2020
2040     PRINT "PLAYER ";J;" LOSES"
2050     A(J)=A(J)-C(J)
2060     GOTO 2090
2070     PRINT "PLAYER " ;J;" WINS ";C(J);" DOLLARS"
2080     A(J)=A(J)+C(J)
2090 RETURN
```

Finally, here is the subroutine corresponding to the bet ODD.

```
3000 'Bet=ODD
3010     K=0
3020     IF X=2*K+1 THEN 3070
3030     K=K+1:IF K>=19 THEN 3040 ELSE 3020
3040     PRINT "PLAYER ";J;" LOSES"
3050     A(J)=A(J)-C(J)
3060     GOTO 3090
3070     PRINT "PLAYER ";J;" WINS ";C(J);" DOLLARS"
3080     A(J)=A(J)+C(J)
3090 RETURN
```

Now we are ready to assemble the subroutines together with the main portion of the program, which is almost the same as before. The only essential alteration is that we must now determine, for each player, which bet was placed.

```
10 CLS
20 RANDOMIZE VAL(RIGHT$(TIME$,2))
30 INPUT "NUMBER OF PLAYERS";N
40 DIM A(5),B(5),C(5)
50 FOR J=1 TO N
60   PRINT "PLAYER ";J
70   INPUT "HOW MANY CHIPS";A(J)
80 NEXT J
90 PRINT "LADIES AND GENTLEMEN! PLACE YOUR BETS PLEASE!"
100 FOR J=1 TO N:          'Place bets
110   PRINT "PLAYER" ;J
120   PRINT "BET TYPE:1=NUMBER BET, 2=EVEN, 3=ODD"
130   INPUT "BET TYPE (1,2, OR 3)";D(J)
```

6.4 Gambling With Your Computer

```
140    IF D(J)=1 THEN 170
150    INPUT "AMOUNT";C(J)
160    GOTO 180
170    INPUT "NUMBER, AMOUNT BET";B(J),C(J)
180 NEXT J
190 X=INT(38*RND+1):   'Spin Wheel
200 CLS
210 PRINT "THE WINNER IS NUMBER";X
220 FOR J=1 TO N:       'Determine winnings and losses
230   ON D(J) GOSUB 1000,2000,3000
240 NEXT J
250 PRINT "PLAYER BANKROLLS"
260 PRINT "PLAYER", "CHIPS"
270 FOR J=1 TO N
280    PRINT J,A(J)
290 NEXT J
300 INPUT "DO YOU WISH TO PLAY ANOTHER ROLL(Y/N)";R$
310 CLS
320 IF R$="Y" OR R$="y" THEN 90
330 PRINT "THE CASINO IS CLOSED. SORRY!"
340 END
1000 'Bet=NUMBER
1010    IF B(J)=X THEN 1050 ELSE 1020
1020    PRINT "PLAYER ";J; " LOSES"
1030    A(J)=A(J)-C(J)
1040    GOTO 1070
1050    PRINT "PLAYER ";J; " WINS"; 32*C(J); "DOLLARS"
1060    A(J)=A(J)+32*C(J)
1070 RETURN
2000    'Bet=EVEN
2010    K=0
2020    IF X=2*K THEN 2070 ELSE 2030
2030    K=K+1: IF K>=20 THEN 2040 ELSE 2020
2040    PRINT "PLAYER ";J;" LOSES"
2050    A(J)=A(J)-C(J)
2060    GOTO 2090
2070    PRINT "PLAYER " ;J;" WINS ";C(J);" DOLLARS"
2080    A(J)=A(J)+C(J)
2090 RETURN
3000    'Bet=ODD
3010    K=0
3020    IF X=2*K+1 THEN 3070 ELSE 3030
3030    K=K+1:IF K>=19 THEN 3040 ELSE 3020
3040    PRINT "PLAYER ";J;" LOSES"
3050    A(J)=A(J)-C(J)
3060    GOTO 3090
3070    PRINT "PLAYER ";J;" WINS ";C(J);" DOLLARS"
3080    A(J)=A(J)+C(J)
3090 RETURN
4000 END
```

Note how the subroutines help to organize our programming. Each subroutine is easy to write and is a small task, and you will have less to think about than when considering the entire program. It is advisable to break a long program into a number of subroutines. Not only is it easier

162 Working With Data

to write in terms of subroutines, but it is much easier to check the program and to locate errors since subroutines may be individually tested.

You may treat the output of the random number generator as you would any other number. In particular, you may perform arithmetic operations on the random numbers generated. For example, 5*RND multiplies the output of the random number generator by 5, and RND+2 adds 2 to the output of the random number generator. Such arithmetic operations are useful in producing random numbers from intervals other than 0 to 1. For example, to generate random numbers between 2 and 3, we may use RND+2.

Example 4. Write a program that generates 10 random numbers lying in the interval from 5 to 8.

Solution. Let us build up the desired function in two steps. We start from the function RND, which generates numbers from 0 to 1. First, we adjust for the length of the desired interval. From 5 to 8 is 3 units, so we multiply RND by 3. The function 3*RND generates numbers from 0 to 3. Now we adjust for the starting point of the desired interval, namely 5. By adding 5 to 3*RND, we obtain numbers lying between 0+5 and 3+5, that is between 5 and 8. Thus, 3*RND+5 generates random numbers between 5 and 8. Here is the program required.

```
10 FOR J=1 TO 10
20    PRINT 3*RND+5
30 NEXT J
40 END
```

Example 5. Write a function to generate random integers from among 5, 6, 7, 8, . . ., 12.

Solution. There are 8 consecutive integers possible. Let us start with the function 8*RND, which generates random numbers between 0 and 8. Since we wish our random number to begin with 5, let us add 5 to get 8*RND+5. This produces random numbers between 5.00000 and 12.9999. We now use the INT function to chop off the decimal part. This yields the desired function:

```
INT(8*RND+5)
```

Exercises (answers on page 374)

Write BASIC functions that generate random numbers of the following sorts.

1. Numbers from 0 to 100.
2. Numbers from 100 to 101.
3. Integers from 1 to 50.
4. Integers from 4 to 80.

5. Even integers from 2 to 50.
6. Numbers from 50 to 100.
7. Integers divisible by 3 from 3 to 27.
8. Integers from among 4, 7, 10, 13, 16, 19, and 22.
9. Modify the dice program so that it keeps track of payoffs and bankrolls, much like the roulette program in Example 2. Here are the payoffs on a bet of one dollar for the various bets:

outcome	payoff
2	35
3	17
4	11
5	8
6	6.20
7	5
8	6.20
9	8
10	11
11	17
12	35

10. Modify the roulette program of Example 2 to check that a player has enough chips to cover the bet.
11. Modify the roulette program of Example 2 to allow for a $100 line of credit for each player.
12. Construct a program that tests one-digit arithmetic facts with the problems randomly chosen by the computer.
13. Make up a list of ten names. Write a program that will pick four of the names at random. (This is a way of impartially assigning a nasty task!)

ANSWERS TO TEST YOUR UNDERSTANDINGS 1, 2, and 3

```
1: 30 percent
2: 10 FOR J=1 TO 50
   20   PRINT INT(2*RND)
   30 NEXT J
   40 END
3: 10 LET X=INT(3*RND + 1)
   20 IF X=1 THEN PRINT "HEADS" ELSE PRINT "TAILS"
   30 END
```

Easing Programming Frustrations

7

166   Easing Programming Frustrations

As you have probably discovered by now, programming can be a tricky and frustrating business. You must first figure out the instructions to give the computer. Next, you must type the instructions into RAM. Finally, you must run the program. Usually after the first run, you must figure out why the program won't work. This process can be tedious and frustrating, especially in dealing with long or complex programs. We should emphasize that programming frustrations often result from the limitations and inflexibility of the computer to understand exactly what you are saying. In talking with another person, you usually sift out irrelevant information, correct minor errors, and still maintain the flow of communication. With a computer, however, you must clear up all of the imprecisions before the conversation can even begin.

Fortunately, your computer has many features designed to ease the programming burdens and to help you track down errors and correct them. We will describe these features in this chapter. We will also present some more tips which should help you develop programs quicker and with fewer errors.

7.1 Flow Charting

In the last three chapters our programs were fairly simple. By the end of Chapter 6, however, we saw them becoming more involved. And there are many programs which are even much more lengthy and complex. You might be wondering how it is possible to plan and execute such programs. The key idea is to reduce large programs to a sequence of smaller programs which can be written and tested separately.

The old saying "A picture is worth a thousand words" is true for computer programming. In designing a program, especially a long one, it is helpful to draw a picture depicting the instructions of the program and their interrelationships. Such a picture is called a **flowchart**.

A flowchart is a series of boxes connected by arrows. Within each box is a series of one or more computer instructions. The arrows indicate the logical flow of the instructions. For example, the flowchart in Figure 7-1 shows a program for calculating the sum $1+2+3+\ldots+100$.

The arrows indicate the sequence of operations. Note the notation "$J=1,2,\ldots,100$" between the second and third boxes. This notation indicates a loop on the variable J. This means that the operation in box 3 is to be repeated 100 times for $J=1, 2, \ldots, 100$. Note how easy it is to proceed from the above flowchart to the corresponding BASIC program:

```
10  S=0                    (box 2)
20  FOR J=1 TO 100
30     S=S+J               (box 3)
40  NEXT J
50  PRINT S                (box 4)
60  END                    (box 5)
```

7.1 Flow Charting

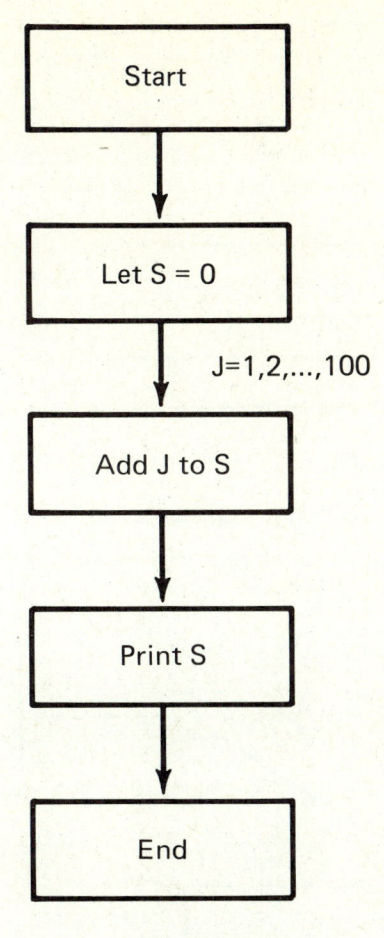

```
        ┌─────────┐
        │  Start  │
        └────┬────┘
             ↓
        ┌─────────┐
        │ Let S=0 │
        └────┬────┘
             ↓  J=1,2,...,100
        ┌─────────┐
        │Add J to S│
        └────┬────┘
             ↓
        ┌─────────┐
        │ Print S │
        └────┬────┘
             ↓
        ┌─────────┐
        │   End   │
        └─────────┘
```

Figure 7-1.

There are many flow charting rules. Different shapes of boxes represent certain programming operations. We will adopt a very simple rule that all boxes are rectangular except for decision boxes. Decision boxes are diamond-shaped. The flowchart in **Figure 7-2** shows a program which decides whether a credit limit has been exceeded.

Note that the diamond-shaped block contains the decision "Is D < L?". Corresponding to the two possible answers to the question are two arrows leading from the decision box. Also note how we used the various boxes to help assign letters to the program variables. Once the flowchart is written, it is easy to transform it into the following program:

```
10   INPUT C                              (boxes 1,2)
20   INPUT D,L
30   D = D + C                            (box 3)
40   IF D>L THEN 100 ELSE 200             (box 4)
```

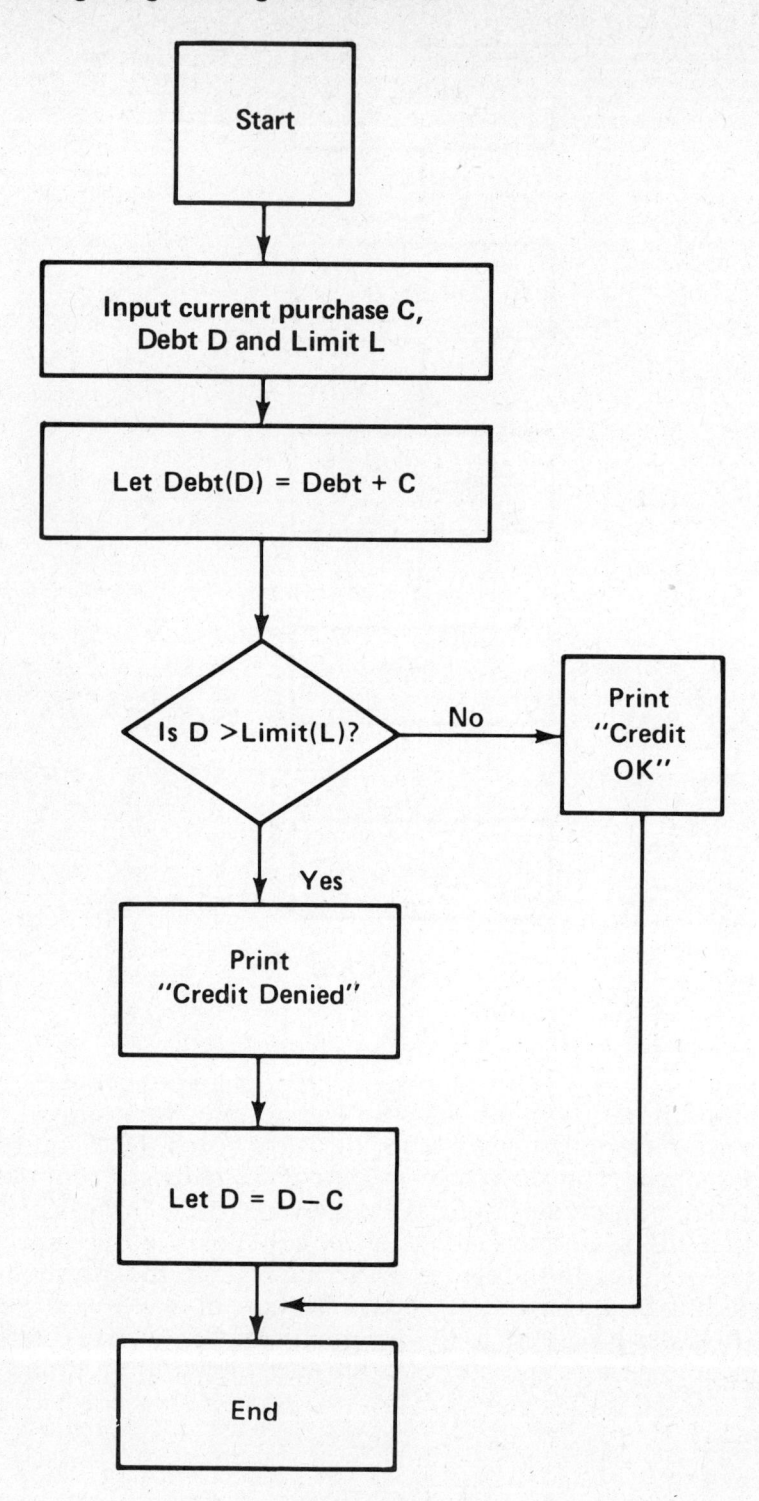

```
┌─────────┐
│  Start  │
└────┬────┘
     │
     ▼
┌─────────────────────┐
│ Input current       │
│ purchase C,         │
│ Debt D and Limit L  │
└────┬────────────────┘
     │
     ▼
┌─────────────────────┐
│ Let Debt(D) = Debt + C │
└────┬────────────────┘
     │
     ▼
   ╱ Is D      ╲   No      ┌──────────┐
  ╱  >Limit(L)? ╲─────────▶│  Print   │
   ╲            ╱          │ "Credit  │
    ╲          ╱           │   OK"    │
     │ Yes                 └────┬─────┘
     ▼                          │
┌─────────────────┐             │
│     Print       │             │
│ "Credit Denied" │             │
└────┬────────────┘             │
     │                          │
     ▼                          │
┌─────────────────┐             │
│  Let D = D – C  │             │
└────┬────────────┘             │
     │◀─────────────────────────┘
     ▼
┌─────────┐
│   End   │
└─────────┘
```

Figure 7-2.

7.1 Flow Charting   169

```
100 PRINT "CREDIT DENIED"      (box 6)
110 D=D-C                      (box 7)
120 GOTO 300                   ("No" arrow)
200 PRINT "CREDIT OK"          (box 5)
300 END                        (box 8)
```

You will find flow charting helpful in thinking out the necessary steps of a program. As you practice flow charting, you will develop your own style and conventions. That's fine. I encourage all personalized touches, as long as they are comfortable and help you write programs.

Exercises (answers on page 376)

Draw flowcharts planning computer programs to do the following.

1. Calculate the sum $1^2 + 2^2 + \ldots + 100^2$, print the result, and determine whether the result is larger than, smaller than, or equal to 487^3.
2. Calculate the time elapsed since the computer was turned on.
3. The roulette program of Section 6.4 (page 158).
4. The payroll program in Example 2 of Section 6.2 (page 143).

7.2 Errors and Debugging

An error is sometimes called a "bug" in computer jargon. The process of finding these errors or "bugs" in a program is called **debugging**. This can often be a ticklish task. Manufacturers of commercial software must regularly repair bugs they discover in their own programs! Your IBM Personal Computer is equipped with a number of features to help detect bugs.

The Trace

Often your first try at running a program results in failure while giving you no indication as to why the program is not running correctly. For example, your program might just run indefinitely, without giving you a clue as to what it is actually doing. How can you figure out what's wrong? One method is to use the **trace** feature. Let us illustrate use of the trace by debugging the following program designed to calculate the sum $1+2+\ldots+100$. The variable S is to contain the sum. The program uses a loop to add each of the numbers 1, 2, 3, ..., 100 to S, which is initially 0.

```
10  S=0
20  J=0
```

170 Easing Programming Frustrations

```
 30  S=S + J
 40  IF J=100 THEN 100 ELSE 200
100  J=J+1
110  GOTO 20
200  PRINT S
300  END
```

This program has two errors in it. (Can you spot them right off?) All you know initially is that the program is not functioning normally. The program runs, but prints out the answer 0, which we recognize as nonsense. How can we locate the errors? Let's turn on the trace function by typing **TRON** (TRace ON) and pressing ENTER. The computer will respond by typing **Ok**. Now type **RUN**. The computer will run our program and print out the line numbers of all executed instructions. Here is what our display looks like:

```
TRON
Ok

RUN
[10] [20] [30] [40] [200] 0
[300]
```

The numbers in brackets indicate the line numbers executed. That is, the computer executes, in order, lines 10, 20, 30, 40, 200, and 300. The zero not in brackets is the program output resulting from the execution of line 200. The list of line numbers is not what we were expecting. Our program was designed (or so we thought) to execute line 100 after line 40. No looping is taking place. How did we get to line 200 after line 40? This suggests that we examine line 40: Lo and behold! There is an error. The line numbers 100 and 200 appearing in line 40 have been interchanged (an easy enough mistake to make). Let's correct this error by retyping the line.

```
 40  IF J=100 THEN 200 ELSE 100
```

In triumph, we run our program again. Here is the output:

```
[10] [20] [30] [40] [100] [110] [20] [30]
[40] [100] [110] [20] [30] [40] [100] [110]
[20] [30] [40] [100]
Break in 110
```

Actually, the above output goes whizzing by us as the computer races madly on executing the instructions. After about 30 seconds, we sense that something is indeed wrong since it is unlikely that our program could take this long. We stop execution by means of the Ctrl-Break key combination. The last line indicates that we interrupted the computer while it was executing line 110. Actually, your screen will be filled with output resembling the above. You will notice that the computer is in a loop. Each time it reaches line 110, the loop goes back to line 20. Why doesn't the loop ever end? In order for the loop to terminate, J must equal 100. Well, can J ever equal 100? Of course not! Every time the computer executes line 20, the value of J is reset to 0. Thus, J is never equal to 100 and line 40 always sends us back to line 20. We clearly don't want to reset J to 0 all the time. After increasing J by 1 (line 100), we wish to add the new J to S. We want to go to 30, not 20. We correct line 110 to read:

```
110 GOTO 30
```

We run our program again. There will be a rush of line numbers on the screen followed by the output 5050, which appears to be correct. Our program is now running properly. We turn off the trace by typing **TROFF** (TRace OFF) and pressing ENTER. Finally, we run our program once more for good measure. The above sequence of operations is summarized in the following display:

```
[40] [200] 5050
[300]
Ok

TROFF
Ok

RUN
5050
Ok
```

In our example above, we displayed all the line numbers executed. For a long program, this may lead to a huge list of line numbers. You may be selective by using TRON and TROFF within your program. Just use them with line numbers, just like any other BASIC instruction. When BASIC encounters a TRON, it begins to display the line numbers executed. When BASIC encounters a TROFF, it stops displaying line numbers. To debug a program, you may temporarily add TRON and TROFF instructions at selected places. As you locate the bugs, remove the corresponding trace instructions.

Error Messages

In the example above the program actually ran. A more likely occurrence is that there is a program line (or lines) that the computer is unable to understand due to an error or some other sort of problem. In this case, program execution ends too soon. The computer can often help in this instance since it is designed to recognize many of the most common errors. The computer will print an error message indicating the error type and the line number in which it occurred. The line with the error is automatically displayed, ready for editing. Suppose that the error reads

```
Syntax Error in 530
530 Y=(X+2(X^2-2)
```

We note that there is an open parenthesis "(" without a corresponding close parenthesis ")". This is enough to trigger an error. We modify line 530 to read

```
530  Y = X + 2 ( X^2 - 2 )
```

We **RUN** the program again and find that there is still a syntax error in line 530! This is the frustrating part since not all errors are easy to spot. However, if you look closely at the expression on the right, you will note that we have omitted the * to indicate the product of 2 and (X^2 − 2). This is a common mistake, especially for those familiar with the use of algebra. (In algebra the product is usually indicated without any operation sign.) We correct line 530 again. (You may either retype the line or use the line editor.)

```
530  Y = X + 2 * ( X^2 - 2 )
```

Now there is no longer a syntax error in line 530!

The next section contains a list of the most common error messages. There are a number of errors not included on our list, especially those associated with disk BASIC. For a complete list of error messages, the reader is referred to the **IBM Personal Computer BASIC Reference Manual**.

Exercises (answers on page 379)

1. Use the error messages to debug the following program to calculate $(1^2 + 2^2 + \ldots + 50^2)(1^3 + 2^3 + \ldots + 20^3)$.

   ```
   10  S = "0"
   20  FOR J = 1 TO 50
   30      S = S + J(2
   40  NEXT K
   50  T = 0
   60  FOR J = 1 TO 20
   70      T = T + J^3
   80  NXT T
   90  NEXT T
   100 A = ST
   110 PRINT THE ANSWER IS, A
   120 END
   ```

2. Use the trace function to debug the following program to determine the smallest integer N for which N^2 is larger than 175263.

   ```
   10  N = 0
   20  IF N^2 < 175263 THEN 100
   30  PRINT "THE FIRST N EQUALS"
   100 N = N + 1
   110 GOTO 10
   200 END
   ```

7.3 Some Common Error Messages

Syntax Error. There is an unclear instruction (misspelled?), mismatched parentheses, incorrect punctuation, illegal character, or illegal variable name in the program.

Undefined line number. The program uses a line number which does not correspond to an instruction. This can easily arise if you delete lines which are mentioned elsewhere. It can also occur when testing a portion of a program that refers to a line not yet written.

Overflow. A number too large for the computer.

Division by zero. Attempting to divide by zero. This may be a hard error to spot. The computer will round to zero any number smaller than the minimum allowed. Use of such a number in subsequent calculations could result in division by zero.

Illegal function call. (For the mathematically-minded.) Attempting to evaluate a function outside of its mathematically defined range. For example, the square root function is defined only for non-negative numbers, the logarithm function only for positive numbers, and the arctangent only for numbers between -1 and 1. Any attempt to evaluate a function at a value outside these respective ranges will result in an illegal function call error.

Missing Operand. Attempting to execute an instruction missing required data.

Subscript Out of Range. Attempting to use an array with one or more subscripts outside the range allowed by the appropriate DIM statement.

String Too Long. Attempting to specify a string containing more than 255 characters.

Out of Memory. Your program will not fit into the computer's memory. This could result from large arrays or too many program steps or a combination of the two.

String Formula Too Complex. Due to the internal processing of your formula, your string formula resulted in a string expression that was too long or complex. This error can be corrected by breaking the string expression into a series of simpler expressions.

Type Mismatch. Attempting to assign a string constant as the value of a numeric variable, or a numeric constant value to a string variable.

Duplicate Definition. Attempting to DIMension an array which has already been dimensioned. Note that once you refer to an array within a program, even if you don't specify the dimensions, the computer will regard it as being dimensioned at 10.

NEXT without FOR. A NEXT statement that does not correspond to a FOR statement.

RETURN without GOSUB. A RETURN statement is encountered while not performing a subroutine.

Out of Data. Attempting to read data that isn't there. This can occur in reading data from DATA statements, cassettes, or diskettes.

Can't Continue. Attempting to give a CONT command after the program has ENDed or before the program has been RUN (such as after an EDIT session).

7.4 Further Debugging Hints

Debugging is something between a black art and a science. Tracking down program bugs can be a very tricky business and to be good at it, you must be a good detective. In the preceding section we listed some of the clues which BASIC automatically supplies, namely the error messages. Sometimes, however, these clues are not enough to diagnose a bug. (For example, your program may run without errors. It may just not do what it is supposed to. In this case, no error messages will be triggered.) In such circumstances you must be prepared to supply your own clues. Here are some techniques.

Insert Extra Print Statements

You may temporarily insert extra PRINT statements into your program to print out the values of key variables at various points in the program. This technique allows you to keep track of a variable as your program is executed.

Insert STOP Commands

It is perfectly possible that your program planning may contain a logical flaw. In this case, it is possible to write a program that runs without error messages, but which does not perform as you expect it to. You may temporarily insert a STOP command to force a halt after a specified portion of the program.

This debugging technique may be used in several ways.

1. When the program encounters a STOP instruction, it halts execution and prints out the line number where the program was stopped. If the program does stop, you will know that the instructions just before the STOP were executed. On the other hand, suppose that the program continues on its merry way. This tells you that the

program is avoiding the instructions immediately preceding the STOP. If you determine the reason for this behavior, then you will likely correct a bug.
2. When the program is halted, the values of the variables are preserved. You may examine them to determine the behavior of your program. (See below for more information.)
3. You may insert several STOP instructions. After each halt, you may note the behavior of the program (line number, values of key variables, and so forth). You may continue execution by typing CONT and pressing ENTER. Note that if you change a program line during a halt, then you may not continue execution, but must restart the program by typing RUN and pressing ENTER.

Examine Variables in the Immediate Mode

When BASIC stops executing your program, the current values of the program variables are not destroyed. Rather, they are still in memory and may be examined as an indication of program behavior. This is true even if the program is halted by means of a STOP instruction or by hitting Ctrl-Break.

Suppose that a program is halted and that the BASIC prompt Ok is displayed. To determine the current values of the program variables INVOICE and FILENAME$, type

```
PRINT INVOICE, FILENAME$
```

and press ENTER. Note that there is no line number. This instruction is in immediate mode. BASIC will display the current values of the two variables, just as if the PRINT statement was contained in a program:

```
 145.83         ACCTPAY.MAR
```

Warning: As soon as you make any alteration in your program (correct a line, add a line), BASIC will reset all the variables. The numeric variables will be reset to zero and the string variables will be set to null. Therefore, if you wish to have an accurate reading of the variable values as they emerge from your program, be sure to request them before making any program changes.

Execute Only a Portion of Your Program

Sometimes it helps to run only a portion of your program. You may start execution at any line using a variation of the RUN command. For example, to begin execution at line 500 type

```
 RUN 500
```

and press ENTER. Note, however, that the RUN command causes all variables to be reset. If some earlier portion of your program sets some variables, then starting the program in the middle may not give an accurate picture of program operation. To get around this problem, you may set variables in immediate mode and start the program using the GOSUB instruction. For example, suppose that the earlier portion of your program set INVOICE equal to 145.83 and FILENAME$ equal to ACCTPAY.MAR. To accurately run a portion of the program depending on these variable values, you would first type

```
INVOICE=145.83:FILENAME$="ACCTPAY.MAR"
```

and press ENTER. (These instructions could be entered on separate lines, each followed by ENTER.) To start the program at line 500, you would then type

```
GOSUB 500
```

and press ENTER. Note that it is not sufficient to use the command

```
RUN 500
```

The RUN command automatically resets the variables.

Your Computer as a File Cabinet

8

178 Your Computer as a File Cabinet

In this chapter we will discuss techniques for using your computer to store and retrieve information.

8.1 What Are Files?

A **file** is a collection of information stored on a mass storage device (diskette, cassette, or hard disk). There are two common types of files: **program files** and **data files**.

Program Files. When a program is stored on diskette, it is stored as a program file. You have already created some program files by saving BASIC programs on diskette. In addition to the programs you create, your DOS diskette contains program files which are necessary to run your computer, such as DOS and the BASIC language.

Data Files. Computer programs used in business and industry usually refer to files of information which are kept in mass storage. For example, a personnel department would keep a file of data on each employee: name, age, address, social security number, date employed, position, salary, and so forth. A warehouse would maintain an inventory for each product with the following information: product name, supplier, current inventory, units sold in the last reporting period, date of the last shipment, size of the last shipment, and units sold in the last 12 months. These files are called *data files*.

Program files and data files are typically stored side by side on the same diskette. And from many points of view, they are the same as far as the computer is concerned. That is, they may be copied, erased, verified, and the procedures are the same for program files as data files. In this chapter we will discuss the procedures for handling files in general and data files in particular.

The computer writes data on the diskette in a form that it can read. We won't worry here about the form in which program files are written. However, it is important to understand the form of data files.

Consider the following example. Suppose that a teacher stores grades in a data file. For each student in the class, there are four exam grades. A typical entry in the data file would contain the following data items:

   student name, exam grade #1, exam grade #2, exam grade #3, exam grade #4

In a data file the data items are organized in sequence, so the beginning of the above data file might look like this:

```
"John Smith", 98, 87, 93, 76, "Mary Young", 99, 78,
87, 91, "Sally Ronson", 48, 63, 72, 80, ...
```

The data file consists of a sequence of string constants (the names) and numeric constants (the grades), with the various data items arranged in a particular pattern (name followed by four grades). This particular arrangement is designed so the file may be read and understood. For instance, if we read the data items above, we know in advance that the data items are in groups of five with the first one a name and the next four the corresponding grades.

In this chapter we will learn to create data files containing information such as the data in the above example. As we shall see, data may be stored in either of two types of data files—sequential and random access. For each type of file we will learn to perform the following operations.

1. Create a data file.
2. Write data items to a file.
3. Read data items from a file.
4. Alter data items in a file.
5. Search a file for particular data items.

8.2 Sequential Files

A **sequential file** is a data file where the data items are accessed in order. That is, the data items are written in consecutive order into the file. The data items are read in the order in which they were written. You may add data items only to the tail end of a sequential file. If you wish to add a data item somewhere in the middle of the file, it is necessary to rewrite the entire file. Similarly, if you wish to read a data item at the end of a sequential file, it is necessary to read all the data items in order and to ignore those that you don't want.

OPENing and CLOSEing Sequential Files

Before you perform any operations on a sequential file, you must first open the file. You should think of the file as being contained in a file cabinet drawer (the diskette). In order to read the file, you must first open the file drawer. This is accomplished using the BASIC instruction **OPEN**. When **OPEN**ing a file, you must specify the file and indicate whether you will be reading from the file or writing into the file. For example, to **OPEN** the file B:PAYROLL for input (for reading the file), we use a statement of the form

```
10 OPEN "B:PAYROLL" FOR INPUT AS #1
```

The #1 is a reference number which we assign to the file when opening it. As long as the file remains open, you may refer to it by its reference number rather than the more cumbersome file specification B:PAYROLL. Here is an alternate form of the instruction for opening a file for input:

```
10 OPEN "I",#1,"B:PAYROLL"
```

(Here the letter "I" stands for "Input".)

180   Your Computer as a File Cabinet

To **OPEN** the file B:GRADES.AUG for output (that is, to write in the file), we use an instruction of the form

```
20 OPEN "B:GRADES.AUG" FOR OUTPUT AS #2
```

Here is an alternate way to write the same instruction:

```
20 OPEN "O",#2,"B:GRADES.AUG"
```

The letter "O" stands for "Output". In Disk BASIC and Advanced BASIC, you may work with three open diskette files at a time. This number may be increased by giving the appropriate command. (More about this procedure later.)

In maintaining any filing system, it is necessary to be neat and organized. The same is true of computer files. A sequential file may be opened for input or for output but not both simultaneously. As long as the file remains open, it will accept instructions (input or output) of the same sort designated when it was opened. To change operations it is necessary to first close the file. For example, to close the file B:PAYROLL in line 10 above, we use the instruction

```
40 CLOSE #1
```

After giving this instruction, we may reopen the file for output using an instruction such as that given in line 20 above. It is possible to close several files at a time. For example, the statement

```
50 CLOSE #5,#6
```

closes the files with reference numbers 5 and 6. We may close all currently open files with the instruction

```
50 CLOSE
```

In a CLOSE statement the # is optional. Thus, it is perfectly acceptable to use

```
50 CLOSE 5,6
```

Good programming practice dictates that all files be closed after use. In any case, the BASIC commands NEW and RUN automatically close any files that might have been left open by a preceding program.

WRITEing Data Items Into a Sequential File

Suppose that we wish to create a sequential file, called INVOICE.001, which contains the following data items.

```
DJ SALES    50357    4    $358.79    4/5/81
```

That is, we would like to write into the file the string constant "DJ SALES" followed by the two numeric constants 50357 and 4, followed by the two string constants "$358.79" and "4/5/81". Here is a program which does exactly that:

8.2 Sequential Files

```
100 OPEN "B:INVOICE.001" FOR OUTPUT AS #1
110 WRITE#1, "DJ SALES", 50357,4,"$358.79", "4/5/81"
120 CLOSE #1
```

The #1 portion of line 110 refers to the identification number given to the file in the OPEN instruction in line 100, namely 1. In a WRITE# statement, a comma must follow the file number.

Note that the **WRITE** instruction works very much like a PRINT statement except that the data items are "printed" in the file instead of on the screen.

While a file is open you may execute any number of WRITE instructions to insert data. Moreover, you may WRITE data items which are values of variables, as in the statement

```
200 WRITE #1, A, A$
```

This instruction will write current values of A and A$ into the file.

Example 1. Write a program to create a file whose data items are the numbers 1, 1^2, 2, 2^2, 3, 3^2, ..., 100, 100^2.

Solution. Let's call the file "SQUARES" and store it on the diskette in drive A:.

```
10 OPEN "A:SQUARES" FOR OUTPUT AS #1
20 FOR J=1 TO 100
30   WRITE#1, J,J^2
40 NEXT J
50 CLOSE #1
60 END
```

Example 2. Create a data file consisting of names, addresses, and telephone numbers from your personal telephone directory. Assume that you will type the addresses into the computer and will tell the computer when the last address has been typed.

Solution. We use **INPUT** statements to enter the various data. Let A$ denote the name of the current person, B$ the street address, C$ the city, D$ the state, E$ the zip code, and F$ the telephone number. For each entry, there is an **INPUT** statement corresponding to each of these variables. The program then writes the data to the diskette. Here is the program:

```
5   OPEN "TELEPHON" FOR OUTPUT AS #1
10  INPUT "NAME"; A$
20  INPUT "STREET ADDRESS"; B$
30  INPUT "CITY"; C$
40  INPUT "STATE"; D$
50  INPUT "ZIP CODE"; E$
60  INPUT "TELEPHONE"; F$
70  WRITE#1, A$, B$, C$, D$, E$, F$
80  INPUT "ANOTHER ENTRY (Y/N)"; G$
90  IF G$="Y" THEN 10
100 CLOSE #1
110 END
```

182   Your Computer as a File Cabinet

You should set up such a computerized telephone directory of your own. It is very instructive. Moreover, when coupled with the search program given below, it will allow you to look up addresses and phone numbers using your computer.

TEST YOUR UNDERSTANDING 1

Use the above program to enter the following address into the file.
John Jones
1 South Main St.
Phila. Pa. 19107
527-1211

TEST YOUR UNDERSTANDING 2

Add to the telephone file started in TEST YOUR UNDERSTANDING 1 above:
Mary Bell
2510 9th St.
Phila. Pa. 19138
937-4896

Reading Data Items

To read items from a data file, it is first necessary to open the file for INPUT (that is, for INPUT to the computer). Consider the telephone file in Example 2. We may open it for input via the instruction

```
300 OPEN "TELEPHON" FOR INPUT AS #2
```

Once the file is open, it may read via the instruction

```
400 INPUT #2, A$,B$,C$,D$,E$,F$
```

This instruction will read six data items from the file (corresponding to one telephone-address entry), assign A$ the value of the first data item, B$ the second, and so forth.

In order to read a file, it is necessary to know the precise format of the data in the file. For example, the form of the above **INPUT** statement was dictated by the fact that each telephone-address entry was entered into the file as six consecutive string constants. The file INPUT statement works like any other INPUT statement: Faced with a list of variables separated by commas, it assigns values to the indicated variables, in the order in which the data items are presented. However, if you attempt to assign a string constant to a numeric variable or vice versa, then BASIC will report an error.

As long as a file is open for INPUT, you may continue to INPUT from it, using as many INPUT statements as you like. These may, in turn, be intermingled with statements that have nothing to do with the file you are reading. Each INPUT statement begins reading the file where the preceding INPUT statement left off.

Here's how to determine if you have read all data items in a file. BASIC maintains the variables EOF(1), EOF(2),. . ., one for each open file. These variables are logical variables. That is, they assume the possible values TRUE or FALSE. You may test for the end of the file using an IF. . .THEN statement. For example, consider the statement

```
100 IF EOF(1) THEN 2000 ELSE 10
```

This statement will cause BASIC to determine if you are currently at the end of file #1. If so the program will go to line 2000. Otherwise, the program will go to line 10. Note that you are not at the end of the file until **after** you read the last data item.

If you attempt to read past the end of a file, BASIC will report an **Input Past End** error. Therefore, before reading a file it is a good idea to determine whether you are currently at the end of the file.

Example 3. A data file, called NUMBERS, consists of numerical entries. Write a program to determine the number of entries in the file.

Solution. Let us keep a count of the current number we are reading in the variable COUNT. Our procedure will be to read a number, increase the count, then test for the end of the file.

```
10 COUNT=0
20 OPEN "NUMBERS" FOR INPUT AS #1
30 IF EOF(1) THEN 100
40 INPUT #1,A
50 COUNT=COUNT+1
60 GOTO 30
100 PRINT "THE NUMBER OF NUMBERS IN THE FILE IS",COUNT
110 CLOSE
120 END
```

Example 4. Write a program which searches for a particular entry of the telephone directory file created in Example 2.

Solution. We will **INPUT** the name corresponding to the desired entry. The program will then read the file entries until a match of names occurs. Here is the program:

```
5   OPEN "TELEPHON" FOR INPUT AS #1
10  INPUT "NAME TO SEARCH FOR"; Z$
20  INPUT #1, A$,B$,C$,D$,E$,F$
30  IF A$=Z$ THEN 100
40  IF EOF(1) THEN 200
50  GOTO 20
100 CLS
110 PRINT A$
120 PRINT B$
```

```
130 PRINT C$,D$, E$
140 PRINT F$
150 GOTO 1000
200 CLS
210 PRINT "THE NAME IS NOT ON FILE"
1000 CLOSE 1
1010 END
```

> **TEST YOUR UNDERSTANDING 3**
>
> Use the above program to locate Mary Bell's number in the telephone file created in TEST YOUR UNDERSTANDINGs 1 and 2.

Example 5. (Mailing List Application) Suppose that you have created your computerized telephone directory, using the program in Example 2. Assume that the completed file is called TELEPHON and is on the diskette in drive A:. Write a program which reads the file and prints out the names and addresses onto mailing labels.

Solution. Let's assume that your mailing labels are the "peel-off" variety, which can be printed continuously on your printer. Further, let's assume that the labels are six printer lines high so that each label has room for five lines of print with one line space between labels. (These are actual dimensions of labels you can buy.) We will print the name on line 1, the address on line 2, the city, state, and zip codes all on line 3, with the city and state separated by a comma.

```
10 OPEN "TELEPHON" FOR INPUT AS #1
20 IF EOF(1) THEN 1000
30 INPUT #1, A$, B$, C$, D$, E$, F$
40 LPRINT A$                :'PRINT NAME
50 LPRINT B$                :'PRINT ADDRESS
60 LPRINT C$;               :'PRINT CITY
70 LPRINT ",";              :'PRINT COMMA
80 LPRINT TAB(10) D$;       :'PRINT STATE
90 LPRINT TAB(20) E$        :'PRINT ZIP CODE
100 LPRINT:LPRINT:LPRINT    :'NEXT LABEL
110 GOTO 20
1000 CLOSE 1
1010 END
```

Adding to a Data File

Here is an important fact about writing data files: Writing a file destroys any previous contents of the file. (In contrast, you may read a file any number of times without destroying its contents.) Consider the file "TELEPHON" created in Example 2 above. Suppose we write a program which opens the file for output and writes what we suppose are additional entries in our telephone directory. After this write operation, the file